A Journey of

Psychic Discovery

*One man's unparalleled 50-year exploration
of Spiritualism and psychic phenomena*

ALAN E. CROSSLEY

First Published 1993 (ISBN 0 9522302 0 8)
This Revised Edition published 2012

Published by
Saturday Night Press Publications,
England
snppbooks@gmail.com
www.snppbooks.com

ISBN 978 1 908421 05 0

Printed by Lightning Source
www.lightningsource.com

www.snppbooks.com

Author's Preface

A Journey of Psychic Discovery includes the details of physical phenomena, spiritual healing and various other aspects of psychic activity taken from a private publication which I wrote in 1974 – *The Enigma of Psychic Phenomena*. As this material is relevant to my fifty years of experience within Spiritualism, psychical research and the paranormal in general some readers may recognize material featured in this earlier work.

Harry Edwards, the well-known healer of the 20th Century wrote the Foreword to the '*Enigma*' book, and Maurice Barbanell, former editor of *Psychic News*, had kindly given permission for extracts from *Psychic News* to be used, including selected photographs.

My appreciation goes also to the late Mrs Susie Hughes for her kind gift to me of several plates showing 'spirit extras' – faces of loved ones manifesting above sitters who sat for William Hope, the well-known spirit photographer in the early part of the century.

Finally, my sincere thanks and deep appreciation to Mr Hems de Winter without whose help and co-operation this book may never have been published.

Alan E. Crossley
1993

Publisher's Preface to this Revised Second Edition

It has given me pleasure to be asked to bring this book back into print.

Alan Crossley was, and still is, highly thought of by many people and the record of his wealth and range of experience deserves to be available for those just starting on their Journey of Discovery.

Because I had available in my personal library a copy of Alan Crossley's original, privately printed *The Enigma of Psychic Phenomena* I have taken the decision to add to this new edition the 'Foreword' written by the renowned healer Harry Edwards for that publication, which Alan acknowledged but omitted from the first edition of this book *A Journey of Psychic Discovery*. Harry Edwards' wise words should be read by as many people as possible, for they are still pertinent thirty-eight years later.

In Chapter 2 a few footnotes have been added to parts of the text, where it is felt that clarification was needed. For historical interest, I have taken the liberty of adding a photograph of a Leslie Flint demonstration in the Kingsway Hall, London, to illustrate a similar occasion which Alan recounted. The photograph is reproduced by permission of Psychic Press Ltd. I have also included a photograph of the author and his sister which was in the original publication.

My thanks also go to Hems de Winter, the original publisher, for allowing me to produce this new edition.

Ann Harrison

Saturday Night Press Publications

July 2012

Dedication

This book is dedicated to my good friend John Kinsella. John was an ardent Spiritualist with particular interest in the work of the National Federation of Spiritual Healers. For some time he was the Vice-Chairman and Treasurer and, together with his colleagues Mr Rafe Owen and Mr Tom Williams, regularly attended the Council meetings ofthe Federation as official representatives of the Lancashire and District Spiritual Healers' Association. Their combined efforts made a practical contribution that was consistently recognised by the then President of the Federation, the late-Mr Harry Edwards, and other members of the Council.

In the early days of the Lancashire Association I had the honour of being its Secretary and, together with the help of Mrs M. Mason, Rafe Owen, Tom Williams and others, we were responsible for arranging the largest ever public demonstration of spiritual healing in Liverpool's Philharmonic Hall by that wonderful trio Mr Harry Edwards with Olive and George Burton – it was a most unforgettable experience. While the crowds flocked toward the hall in a driving snowstorm, John was inside with his team, putting the finishing touches to a mammoth task of organisation. The result of this meeting attracted many new members interested in the work of healing and gave the Lancashire Association the boost it needed to go forward at that time. Its progress was maintained for many years.

John Kinsella will be remembered for his utter dedication and loyalty. He was a wise man with a sense of humour, often unpredictable and exasperating at times. His philosophy was simple, his faith in the 'spirit world' unshakable! We often disagreed about the philosophical implications of psychic phenomena but he was always magnanimous and would sit back and roar with laughter whenever I suggested an alternative explanation to the Spiritualist hypothesis of an after-life.

Although John was aware of my varying views, he was tolerant toward them. He also knew that one day I would write about my experiences and advance some of the ideas we used to discuss. The least I can say in respect of John is that my life was enriched, as indeed was that of all who had the good fortune to know this kind and warm-hearted man. It was through his competent guidance and wise leadership that I was able to develop my own psychic faculties, in a circle to which I was proud to belong and from which its members have since gone forth in varying capacities to help others in the propagation of the Truth concerning psychic and spiritual matters.

ALAN E. CROSSLEY

Contents

Illustrations

Introduction

by way of a prologue the following provides
a glimpse of my childhood

The Broken Road

I was born 26th October 1924 on the stairs (so my mother told me) leading to a one-roomed attic in the slums of Manchester. My first memory was this attic – it had a one window, a skylight which leaked. The room was dark, bare and cold with no furniture or floor covering on the floorboards, biscuit tins and orange boxes comprised the furniture.

My father was a bookbinder by trade and an accomplished organist, but this was a time of depression. The sound of his footsteps as he climbed the stairs to the attic had a hollow echo that excited me. I loved my dad – I felt secure when he came home. He would take off his bowler hat and stroke the nap in a circular motion and hang it on a nail.

My mother always sat on a tiny chair, as one would find in a children's nursery – this chair followed her for years whenever we moved. The attic was rented at one shilling per week (5p today). In retrospect we were very poor and always hungry. The '20s and '30s affected a lot of folk. I remember well a black Valor paraffin heater, always with a pan of water on it, which stood close to where my mother sat. The heater was turned so low it burned with a yellow flame, the smell from it compensated somewhat for the lack of heat it gave off.

Mother had a bed in one corner. My sister Eileen and I slept together in another corner on the floorboards with old clothes for cover. Food, except what mother ate, was non-existent, as was any kind of domestic activity in the way of cleaning and preparation of meals as was usual in other households. Eileen and I would pick up orange peel and any other edible matter we could find from the gutters and rubbish bins. Mother of course knew this, but it sufficed to keep us going.

One day as a 'treat', mother poured some warm water from the pan on the paraffin stove into some aluminium bowls, the kind used for boiling puddings. "Put some salt and pepper in the water" she said, "it will bring the flavour out!" As I look back on this, I think of Oliver Twist, he at least got a bowl of gruel – and had the cheek to ask for more!

In those days there was no Social Security as we know it today. What did exist was something called the 'Guardians' and because my father had no work, they supplied a 'food note' to obtain basic food such as bread, margarine and potatoes – the items were listed and the shopkeeper claimed the money from the 'Guardians'.

At the age of five I was sent to a Children's Home in Frodsham, Cheshire, with my brother John. It was a place for destitute children suffering from malnutrition, but it was lovely. We slept in a proper bed with sheets and blankets and had a bath for the first time! We had three meals a day and for supper, a glass of milk and a Chelsea bun. I remember licking the syrup off the top of the bun and picking the currants from it. Life was good, we put on weight, went swimming and enjoyed school – it was all so new and exciting – to eat, sleep in a bed and feel warm. What luxury!

The rest of my childhood was spent in homes. One was Styal Cottage Homes near Wilmslow in Cheshire (now a woman's prison). Styal was a turning point in my life. I learned to read and write – hated arithmetic. Styal was self-supporting with its own farmlands, bakery, laundry, school, church and a 52-piece silver band. I was in the choir and sang descant – whatever that meant! At nine years of age,

I won a swimming certificate at Styal and have it to this day.

I worked on the farm, in the bakery and the laundry in turn. John was in the band and played a 'kettle drum'. The band won the colours at Belvue, Manchester, competing against professional men bands. I was proud of it and the fact that John was a drummer in the band. Imagine it: none of the players was over twelve years-of-age. It said something for the bandmaster who was a strict disciplinarian. I was made to scrub the wooden floor of the band room once for talking on the way to school. That bandmaster always escorted us to school, in uniform and a handle-bar moustache, slowly riding a bicycle.

At the age of twelve I was sent to a boys' home in Chelmsford, Essex, until I was fourteen. It was during my time at Chelmsford that I heard my mother, who was living at Southend-on-Sea, had cracked her skull falling off a bicycle and was in Southend General Hospital. We had threepence a week pocket money. One Saturday, when I had got my threepence, I ran away from the home with the object of seeing my mother. With threepence in my pocket, I ran, walked and got a lift. I saw a beggar and gave him a penny, bought a penny rock cake to eat on the way and an orange to give my mother when I got to the hospital. On arrival at the hospital, a commissionaire chased me and tried to stop me, but I was not to be deterred and followed the signs to Victoria Ward.

On entering, a nurse said: "Where are you going?" I ignored her as I saw a figure sitting up in bed with the head covered in bandages, it was Mother. As I gave her the orange, she said: "What are you doing here?" I squeezed her hand. "I've run away to see you," I said. Then a policeman walked up to me and dragged me away. It had been reported that I was missing from the home. They must have guessed where I had gone. I was taken in comfort by car back to Chelmsford.

At the age of fourteen I left Chelmsford, fitted out in a suit with long trousers and a suitcase. I was taken to a Hostel in Tulse Hill, Brixton, London. A job had been secured for me with Gaumont British Film Corporation in Regent Street, London, in the postal department at 7/6d per week (35p at today's rate). With no parental support or anyone behind me to give me a push, I faced the big wide world alone.

I took the tram from Brixton to Westminster Bridge, walked across Horse Guards Parade, through Downing Street, up the Haymarket and into Piccadilly for Regent Street. I was delivering the mail to the various offices of Gaumont British and as I was leaving the office of Mark Ostra, the Boss, he called me back, asked my name and told me to go. Later that day I was asked to see a man who told me that Mark Ostra had noticed me and thought I would be suitable as an 'extra' in the film 'Goodbye Mr. Chips' with Greer Garson and Robert Donat. Imagine – me in a film!

However, it was not to last, I wrote to Mother excitedly and told her the news, thinking she would be pleased. Instead she wrote me a long letter saying it wasn't the kind of life for me; that London was a den of iniquity and I should go home to Southend. The move proved to be disastrous. No job, no meals, nothing had changed so far as Mother was concerned. Life was wretched and miserable, it was as if my mother did not want me to succeed at anything. She once said she would see us all off and the most terrible remark I will always remember was when in a moment of anger she declared: "I don't know how I bore such a viper as you."

Apparently mother had a 'hit list' and ticked off each one in the family as they died of one thing or another. First was my sister Eileen – she committed suicide in Australia, her husband having left her high and dry with two boys, Phillip and David. Things were too much for her. When I got the news of Eileen from a neighbour, I travelled from Liverpool to Southend to give my mother the news. After telling her that Eileen was dead, she casually remarked: "Oh, I thought John would have gone before Eileen!" I felt sick at her cold, hard manner.

John died in a Cheshire Home with chronic arthritis, hastened by the prolonged use of the drug Cortisone. My brother Ralph died of alcohol poisoning, then my Dad with cancer of the throat. He was picked up wandering the streets of London in a delirious state and had gone down to less than five stone.

Mother died some years later from cancer of the stomach, refusing to have a doctor or to enter hospital. I understood she died a terrible death.

Apart from a half sister living in London, I am the sole survivor of the Crossley family. However, I think I know why, and so will the reader as you follow my Journey of Discovery and see how a Higher Power can work in one's life – overcoming all adversity.

After my Dad died, Mother sent me a black leather satchel with a piece of coal inside and a poem he had written to her. That was all they found on him when he was picked up in London, a dying man. The poem went missing but I remember the last line vividly. It read: 'The only thing left between us is a broken road that leads from me to you.'

The author aged 5, while resident at a children's home in Frodsham, Cheshire

Chapter 1

Seeking the Truth

The purpose of this book is not to question the existence of supernormal phenomena, or to prove one way or the other the basis upon which many people believe in an after-life. Neither does it seek to prove or disprove the claim that through such phenomena they are able to communicate with those who have died.

The aim is to present the evidence of personal experience and then to express some personal views as to the nature and causes underlying the many and varied phenomena demonstrated through mediumship.

The author is able to draw upon a wealth of knowledge gained over a period of fifty years and has made an intensive study of the subject, witnessing both genuine and fraudulent demonstrations by people of greater or lesser ability, psychic and otherwise.

A more recent example of psychic phenomena to arouse controversy is provided by the advent of Uri Geller with his ability to bend metal simply by stroking the surface gently with his finger. His equally remarkable demonstration of telepathic powers indicate both mental and physical mediumship. These faculties have been developed and used by many people throughout the centuries for various purposes, mainly in a Spiritualistic sense where responsibility for the phenomena is attributed to discarnate entities inhabiting the 'spirit world'. Whether there is truth in this idea or whether the phenomena can be accounted for by other causes is a question that, in my opinion, has still not been finally settled. The controversy will continue until a concerted effort is made by science to investigate the whole subject on a rational basis and without prejudice.

In order to believe in anything, a good deal of understanding is necessary and it is precisely the lack of knowledge and understanding of the true nature and forces involved regarding mediumship and its function that relatively very few people can, with certainty, attribute the phenomena to a specific cause. It is one thing to say "I know" and another to say "I believe", yet much of the evidence regarded as proof by Spiritualists and their hypothesis of an after-life could well have other explanations.

From the time modern Spiritualism made its advent in 1848 in the small town of Hydesville, Rochester, U.S.A. where the Fox sisters were reported to have produced supernormal phenomena, there have been periods of renewed interest and curiosity, especially between the wars. Various appliances are produced to aid 'communication' with the spirit world, such as planchettes and ouija boards. Experiments with these appliances often prove to be fruitless and frustrating and seldom provide anything more than an hour's entertainment.

However, Spiritualism, with its demonstrable phenomena, has become one of the most controversial subjects of modern times. It owes much of its success and growth to both the gullible and the intelligent, for its adherents are drawn from all walks of life. The distinct lack of discipline within its ranks is, in my opinion, one of its greatest weaknesses, not only attracting idle curiosity but also frauds and charlatans whose main purpose is to exploit people who seek comfort and assurance from those claiming the ability to contact the departed.

It is significant that following the end of two world wars, a tremendous surge of interest in Spiritualism emerged. This, I believe, was due to the huge loss of life and the need of so many relatives to seek evidence of their loved ones from beyond the grave. One cannot underestimate the highly emotional aspect of this need, as the desire to believe in an after-life must be at its strongest point following the death of a loved one. Large halls throughout the country were packed to capacity after the last war to hear celebrated mediums giving clairvoyance. Astounding messages purporting to come from the dead were eagerly accepted as evidence of the survival of sons and fathers who lost their lives in action.

However, it is my purpose to describe the phenomena which I have personally witnessed in as impartial a manner as possible, avoiding any attempt to arrive at a final conclusion as to their origin, nature or cause. The authenticity of the phenomena described in the following chapters must inevitably lead to many questions. The implications behind what appear to be intelligent control of forces, as yet little understood, will require honest and patient investigation by men of science.

There is little doubt that mediumistic phenomena do not, as yet, fulfil the requirements of science, simply because of their character and the inability of mediums to guarantee repetitive results. Also, the fact that such phenomena defy rational explanation is because they may well be governed by laws outside those at present known to science. The present attitude of science is still largely a negative one, though there is a growing tendency towards taking a cautious look at it.

The reason for science's lack of interest in the past is due to the fact that it refused to admit the reality of such phenomena. A healthy scepticism or reasoned opposition would command more respect coming from those who, in the first instance, have made a special study of mediumship rather than from those with opinions based on ignorance.

Whatever the opposition, whether it be from science or the Church, the Spiritualist hypothesis is that through the demonstration of mediumship, including clairvoyance, physical phenomena, psychic art and healing, etc., it is possible to communicate with a spirit world. After all, no one has been able to disprove the claims of Spiritualists. At the same time, no other group or body of people attempt to provide the evidence that it is possible for the dead to communicate under prescribed conditions.

The question is – do the phenomena and the accompanying evidence justify an unquestioning belief in a life after death. Opinions differ and it depends on what is regarded as evidence as well as on whether that evidence can be explained in some other way.

I know of people who have experienced some remarkable phenomena and have been so obsessed with fraud that they put this forward to account for it. The fact is that they preclude the possibility of any genuine phenomena and, like the ostrich, bury their heads in the sand and cry that they can see nothing! The late Professor C.E.M. Load once said of an experience he had while staying the night at a haunted house (a piece of soap was hurled at him by an unseen agency) "I saw it happen, but I don't believe it." How much more difficult must it be for someone who has not seen to believe?

Perhaps the reader may be guided by the words of Frederick the Great when he said: "I seek the truth everywhere and respect it whenever I find it and submit to it whenever it is shown to me."

My interest in the occult was first aroused after reading a copy of *Psychic News* which had been left on the seat of a train. Inside the newspaper was reference to a book entitled *My Talks with the Dead* by Hannen Swaffer, a Fleet Street journalist of repute. He was commonly known as 'The Pope of Fleet Street', a Socialist and ardent believer in Spiritualism. The article impressed me because I had always held Hannen Swaffer to be a man of sound judgment and though cynical in some things, was forthright in what he believed in, whether it was politics or anything else. The book, which I obtained and read carefully, revealed a whole new world of activity and was sufficient to warrant a personal effort to find out more about the subject of the psychic world and those who engaged in supernormal practices.

I remember when I was quite young my mother describing her experience with mediums and how, at the séances she attended, the dead of the 1914-1918 war returned from the grave to communicate messages to their loved ones. She spoke of ectoplasm, trumpets, ouija boards, materialisations, transfigurations and clairvoyance. She told me that she had the 'gift' of 'second sight' and could do what the mediums did. However, she avoided its practice, she said, because it took too much out of her. On one occasion she looked into a black mirror and was in a trance for three days!

It was during the war of 1939-45 whilst in the forces that I had what you might call my first glimpse of the future. I suppose it could be termed a psychic experience. Just prior to the invasion of Normandy, I was in a concentration area awaiting embarkation. The night before we were due to embark for France I had a vivid dream, along with others, I was in some kind of amphibious tank crossing a river. When we reached the other side, heavy shelling prevented us from leaving the craft. I looked over the side and clearly saw my Commanding Officer, who had been in the forward craft, being carried away by some medical orderlies; his leg was badly injured and bleeding.

The next morning I told some of my comrades in the barrack room of the dream I had. They laughed it off, suggesting that I must have had too much ale in the NAAFI the night before! Yet, a few days after arriving in Normandy, my unit was attached to a special armoured division. It employed various new and unique vehicles, among which were a number of amphibious craft called Buffaloes. These were designed to plough through water, propelled by tank tracks. Their purpose was to ferry troops across rivers where the bridges had been destroyed. I had not seen any equipment like this in England as it was secret up to the time of 'D' Day. Orders came for us to move across the river. We arrived in the evening and I shall never forget it as long as I live. The place was swarming with mosquitoes, causing havoc to everyone. They did more to undermine morale than anything the enemy could do!

It was early the next morning when the assault was to be made. Several Buffaloes were brought to the river bank into which we trooped. As our barrage of artillery opened up, we moved across the river under its cover. It was at this point that I realised this was, in fact, part of the dream I had before leaving England. Enemy shells began to fall round us as we reached the bank on the other side of the river. I remember peeping over the side of the craft and there, within seconds of disembarking, I noticed two medical orderlies lifting the Commanding Officer on to a stretcher. He had been badly injured and his leg was bleeding.

Later, I caught up with some of my colleagues to whom I had mentioned the dream back home. "What about too much NAAFI ale now?" I asked, to which one chap remarked, "Blimey, the man must be psychic!"

Several incidents of precognition featured during my service on the Continent and I am convinced that because of them I was able to take precautions which enabled me to come through the whole war unscathed. For instance, three of us were billeted in a Dutch farmhouse and were sleeping in the loft. After the first night I had a premonition that the house would collapse. I did not want to alarm anyone unduly but suggested that we slept in the local school in future, rather than in the farmhouse, so that when enemy fighters strafed the village, as had happened once or twice before, the school would afford greater protection.

The first night in the school was quite peaceful, but the next night a doodlebug (a V.1) on its way to England suddenly went berserk and cut out over the village. The farmhouse received a direct hit and was demolished. The school suffered only superficial damage as a result of blast. Coincidence? Well, maybe. The fact is that I was impelled to heed some kind of warning and I am alive to tell the tale!

After returning to England in 1946 I obtained a position as a civilian with a paint manufacturer who trained me to be a demonstrator. The job took me to several parts of the country and it was during this time that I noticed several advertisements for clairvoyance. The meetings were open to the public and admission was by ticket only. One of the outstanding clairvoyants at that time was Ronald Strong. I went to see him demonstrate on several occasions. His clairvoyance was impressive and the confidence of the man was such that he would never take no for an answer. Most of the details of his messages were macabre as well as tragic. The point was that the recipients of the messages claimed the details as correct, even when the spirit purporting to communicate had died by putting their head in a gas oven or had been trampled to death by a horse. The impact upon the audience from such 'evidence' was dramatic.

After observing several of these demonstrations it became quite obvious that here was a faculty that could not be dismissed lightly. Telepathy? – Well, in a way, I suppose it was. The question arises: is the information the medium gives telepathy from the living or the dead? Taken on face value, I can understand why so many people are prepared to accept the messages as coming from the deceased or some other discarnate source. In the absence of proof either way, one cannot be dogmatic as to the true source of such information. That it serves to boost the morale of most people on the receiving end of a message is clear and undeniable.

Still on the trail to find out more about the subject, I obtained a book entitled *The Mediumship of Jack Webber* by Harry Edwards, the famous healer. It was a remarkable book dealing with the physical phenomena of the séance room. There were several photographs recording various phenomena taken with infra-red film illustrating ectoplasmic formations, levitation, trumpet phenomena and an extraordinary case of the removal of the medium's jacket by supernormal means. (Mr Edwards kindly gave me permission to reproduce this photograph. Careful study will show a situation normally impossible to produce (see page 57).

Personal experience of this type of phenomena through a similar medium, though not quite so advanced as Jack Webber, is dealt with in a later chapter. After I read Harry Edwards' book I knew that here was a phase of mediumship which could provide something tangible, even if it did appear out of this world! The difficulty, as I soon realised, was the rarity of this kind of phenomena and it was not going to be easy to find a 'circle' where I would be admitted to observe the phenomena for myself.

The question so often asked by people when hearing about happenings as those described in Harry Edwards' book is why there is not more publicity given to the phenomena; why have we not heard of such things before and what is science doing about it? These and many other points are dealt with later.

As I have already indicated, my purpose is firstly to present the evidence and describe the various phenomena that I have been privileged to witness and then attempt to give some idea as to the causes and nature of the phenomena and their possible implications so far as the future of man is concerned. It is my opinion that the veil has only been partially lifted on the deeper regions of the psychic and it would seem that there is a vast reservoir still to be discovered as to the true purpose and potential of the human brain and its unknown regions. It has been recognised for some time now that certain areas of the brain exist which as yet have no apparent purpose or use. The fact that they do exist, points to some future activity in which their operation may be vital.

It is my opinion that some people have developed a portion of these areas of the brain through which the faculties of the psychic operate. Science, it seems, will have to adopt a completely new approach. Instead of concentrating on the purely physical aspect of nature and the laws which govern it, its attention will be directed toward a field of activity where certain laws operate that are not new but need to be discovered and recognised if the pattern of the universe is to present a more complete picture.

The phenomena most people are familiar with, so far as the psychic aspect of man is concerned, are card guessing, dowsing, pendulum swinging and ESP experiments. Other trivial experiments, such as the use of an upturned glass for spelling out 'messages' which purport to come from discarnate sources and the employment of an ouija board as an alternative method for the same purpose, are looked upon with disdain and are invariably a diversion. It is the prominence given to such basic and unreliable experiments that has caused the subject to remain in the realm of fantasy. They have therefore provided little scope for serious study or attention. Only the more advanced forms of phenomena demand recognition. They are the result of laws, not contradictory but complementary to the existing laws governing the physical world as already established by science.

Man is constantly increasing his knowledge and must continue to face the challenge presented to him by the emergence of phenomena outside the accepted range of understanding. To refuse to meet this challenge is highly irresponsible and can only delay progress toward a more enlightened human society. Many of man's problems, particularly in the psychological field, in psychosomatic illness and in other mental aberrations could well find a solution in a greater understanding of the psychic nature of man.

Perhaps many of the patients of our mental hospitals are there simply because we know so little about the function of the psyche and that, as more is known, we can begin to see a measure of progress to diminish the ever increasing numbers being admitted to institutions for the mentally subnormal. Drugs and physical approaches may produce a temporary change or depress the symptoms. Like most medicines that are prescribed, they only serve to relieve the symptoms rather than address the cause of the illness.

One form of mediumship which is practised fairly widely is that of psychic and spiritual healing. It is becoming more accepted as a result of the enormous number of people who have responded to it after medical science has failed. Surely this illustrates the value it makes toward the healing of the whole person instead of the purely physical aspect? This facet of mediumship is dealt with more fully in the chapter on healing.

I would first like to deal with the kind of phenomena that is commonly called 'physical'. With this I include telekinesis, apports, materialisation, direct voice and levitation. I have been most fortunate to experience all of these at one time or another through different mediums. The conditions for their production, basically, are usually the same. Some mediums, of course, are more developed than others and are therefore capable of advanced and more intricate phenomena. Many fall short, while others are uninhibited by factors such as scepticism or criticism.

Much has to do with the mental and physical make-up of the medium and his chemistry, especially in the production of ectoplasm in the case of materialisation phenomena. What I have realised about this kind of mediumship is that it is clearly vulnerable to unwarranted interference, with the result that the medium suffers physical harm and in some cases, death. It is not surprising, therefore, that when a medium of this type has spent many years sitting in order to develop the mediumship, they are most careful whom they invite to witness the phenomena. It is unlikely they would jeopardise the whole thing, including the risk of personal injury, by inviting unscrupulous or ignorant persons whose motives are suspect.

Incidentally, I have seen the result of this behaviour and the consequences arising from it and I cannot stress the importance of adhering to a strict code of conduct in the interest of the medium's mental and physical wellbeing. From my knowledge of Spiritualism I have cause to condemn many within its ranks for their treatment and abuse of mediums. This stems more from ignorance, but I cannot accept the indifference and lack of concern shown in the past toward the fate of mediums who have been maltreated and their 'gift' exploited by a minority who sought nothing more than monetary gain.

Even ordinary, decent standards have been ignored for the sake of expediency. I have known a physical medium, after a séance, left to walk miles to the nearest station in order to travel back home without even a cup of tea! Anyone who knows or understands the mechanics of mediumship would take greater care to see that mediums are catered for properly and protected far more than they have been in the past, especially if they want to enjoy the benefits such mediumship provides.

It is my opinion that because of the lack of consideration, mediums of this kind are becoming increasingly rare. Not only is it extremely difficult to gather a handful of people who are willing to sit indefinitely or for as long as it is necessary to enable a potential medium to develop, it is also virtually impossible to provide the competent leadership and guidance necessary for successful development.

It is to the credit of the pioneers that the following descriptions relating to séances I attended proved to be so rewarding and satisfactory. The level of phenomena was the result of years of patience, consistency in sitting and a number of other factors involving sacrifices on the part of the sitters involved. Loyalty too was a necessary ingredient to encourage the medium to pursue a long and often tedious process of development. The results were only matched by the effort put in by the collective contribution of the sitters. Unless a group is prepared for the slog and all that is required to enable a potential medium to realise the fruits of his or her innate faculty, its members may as well avoid wasting their own, as well as the prospective medium's time.

The following chapter, however, will indicate to the reader just how such a 'circle' succeeded in its objective and the various phenomena that manifested. What I must emphasise, of course, is that to describe something does not explain it. Better men than I cannot fully explain or understand this most complex subject. What I can say is that I have seen what I have seen with my normal faculties of reason, observation and intelligence. It will not do for anyone to suggest that I was hypnotised, suffering from hallucinations, or that I was simply a gullible fool. At the same time, I reserve my opinion as to the real causes behind the phenomena, whether they are indeed, as some believe, due to discarnate intelligence, or in some subtle way emanate from the untapped and hidden reservoir of the medium's unconscious ability. Time alone will reveal the truth, dependent, of course, on how determined man is in his search for it.

The Author with his sister Rose, who witnessed a great deal of the phenomena described in this book.

Chapter 2

Physical Mediumship

The Mediumship of Mrs M.R.Gunning

Mrs Gunning was a well-built woman with a genial but shrewd personality. When she looked at you she seemed to see through the exterior and I will always remember my first meeting with her. After scrutiny, I was relieved when she gave her approval to join her circle on a probationary basis. In turn, I tried to assure her that I would observe all the requirements of such a circle. "I know you will," she said. "I would not have invited you otherwise!" Her smile reassured me and instinctively I knew that we were 'en rapport' from the beginning.

It was my mother who introduced me to this medium. She had already been attending Mrs Gunning's circle for some time and since it was held in her own home – a semi-detached house in the suburbs of Southend-on-Sea, Essex – it was convenient, as I lived in Rayleigh, only about three miles away.

Mrs Gunning was a physical medium. She told me that she had sat for fifteen years and had been fortunate in having loyal and steadfast sitters which enabled her development to reach a very high standard. She paid tribute to her husband, who was also a medium in his own right. He conducted regular healing sessions which I attended as an observer on several occasions.

On the evening of the séance, which was held every Wednesday at eight o'clock prompt, I was shown into a small room. This room was set aside specifically for the purpose and was permanently blacked out. The only illumination was a tiny red light in front of a black curtain which stretched across one corner of the room. Behind the curtain was a stout bentwood chair in which the medium sat during the séance.

There was no furniture in the room other than nine plain wooden chairs. The floor was covered with linoleum and the walls were plain. On the floor to the right of the medium's chair were a number of items. These consisted of a trumpet (a cone-shaped metal megaphone), a tambourine, two luminous plaques and a jug of cold water.

The sitters were beginning to arrive. Mrs Gunning entered the room and sat down between the curtains. As the final sitter took their place in the circle, the medium welcomed everybody and proceeded to give a short talk, warning of the dangers to herself should anyone be tempted to interfere with the proceedings and assuring us that there was nothing to fear during the séance.

While this preliminary discussion was taking place, the items on the floor by the medium's feet began to bob about of their own accord! The time was approaching eight o'clock and I felt a distinct atmosphere building up. Suddenly, Mrs Gunning turned and looked down at the various appliances, now jumping about the floor. "Will you please stop that," she said, almost admonishingly, "The séance has not begun yet!" Evidently the spirits were congregating and eager to start. Whatever the explanation, it was quite obvious that nothing short of supernormal activity could account for this impromptu display before the light was put off!

At eight o'clock sharp, Mrs Gunning asked for the door to be locked and the light to be switched off. The room was in total darkness. Only the eerie glow of the luminous plaques and trumpets could be seen emitting an aura of light near the medium. Her breathing became heavy as she slipped into a trance. At this point one of the sitters burst forth into flat and tuneless rendering of *Onward Christian Soldiers*. Gradually we all joined in, but it seemed a poor welcome for those from the 'other side' to be greeted by, some singing in a different key from the others. The temperature in the room had dropped considerably, always an indication that phenomena was about to take place.

The cold air wafted around my face and legs. Suddenly, the trumpet swept up from the floor toward the ceiling and gyrated above our heads at great speed. While this was happening, a large mass, spherical in shape with a fluorescence of its own, hovered about eye level in the centre of the circle. This strange ball of light fluctuated in density until it became extremely bright so as to make the sitters visible. I glanced up to catch sight of the trumpet whizzing around high above our heads. The mass of stuff slowly moved close to one of the sitters and began to pulsate like a sponge being squeezed. Everyone felt a fine spray of water, slightly perfumed, descend upon them. Then the trumpet came down from the ceiling and remained suspended in front of a sitter. As this happened, the strange mass disappeared.

The trumpet wobbled as it hovered in front of the sitter. The singing stopped abruptly and simultaneously a powerful voice issued from the wide end. The sitter responded, "You are very welcome, God bless you." The conversation which took place between the voice from the trumpet and the sitter was quite normal, except that the voice speaking from the trumpet belonged to a relative who had died several years ago! The sitter did not appear to doubt or question the identity of the person purporting to speak. In fact, what impressed me at the time was the blasé manner in which the sitter accepted the situation. Quite obviously they were accustomed to such an experience. This exercise was repeated several times, involving different sitters, each one apparently enjoying a chat and joke with a discarnate relative!

The mechanics behind this phenomena, known as the direct voice, is a complex one. It would appear that a 'voice box' is constructed, something similar to a temporary larynx. It is believed that 'chemists' from the spirit world are responsible for blending various substances taken from the medium and sitters to produce a physical counterpart of the larynx once used by the spirit when in the body on earth. The intelligence of the spirit is brought to bear upon this and vibrated so as to produce the audible sound of speech. This theory may be over simplified since it must be a much more complex process than we care to realise.

In the case of Mrs Gunning, a connecting link of ectoplasmic ribbon from her solar plexus connected the narrow end of the trumpet. The elasticity of this ribbon enabled the trumpet to reach out to any sitter in the circle. However crude the process appears to be, I think it should be realised that the mechanism is, in fact, both temporary and constructed in a matter of a few seconds. That it serves its purpose is the more important issue. The levitation of the trumpet, for instance, while moving at great speed, diving in and out between the sitters' heads, at no time collided with anyone in the room. I, personally, felt its effect as it flew past my ears. The air was intensely cold.

As the séance proceeded the trumpet directly faced me. I think I froze for a moment, wondering who was going to speak. Faintly, a voice issued forth: "Hello Alan."

"Hello," I replied a little nervously. "You will never guess who this is," said the voice. "I cannot guess who you are," I replied, "but I would be very pleased to know." There was an embarrassed silence for a moment. "It's Tommy," said the voice. The trumpet moved over to my mother sitting next to me. "Hello Mum, isn't this wonderful, I bet you never thought I could do this. Give my love to Ralph, Eileen and John." I listened intently as my mother did the talking. "I will," she said. After a brief pause Tommy continued: "Ga is here too, she sends her love to you all and will try and speak to you next time, but there is someone else here who wants to speak, you know who he is, Mum, his name is Abdul. I'll say goodbye now and let him speak." The trumpet moved close to my mother's face and, with what sounded like a kiss, Tommy withdrew.

The trumpet rose a little higher as the next voice spoke. I could not understand what was said, but my mother did. The voice was that of Abdul Bahá, the distinguished Bahá'í Leader. His words, spoken in Arabic, were the Bahá'í greeting which he gave to all whom he met. The communication was brief, with a promise that he would attempt to materialise at some future date. This undertaking was given by the Medium's Guide, who often intervened with comments following the person who had communicated. My mother was decidedly impressed that Abdul Bahá should honour her with his presence. No-one in that room knew of her association with the Bahá'í Movement and I doubt if any of the sitters had ever heard of it before. A sequel to this occasion appears later on in this book, so I will let the matter rest for the time being.

Returning to the communication from 'Tommy'. This was a remarkable incident. Tommy was a twin brother to my sister Rose. He had been dead for sixteen years. His reference to my sister Eileen and brothers Ralph and John was made quite spontaneously. Again, no-one to my knowledge knew the names of my family, particularly the medium whom I had met for the first time that evening. We always referred to our grandmother as 'Ga'. Even my mother was surprised at such evidence. As she said to me afterwards, "Ga would never have any truck with Spiritualism at any price!"

What can one say about such an experience? It all seemed so normal! My mind would go to those outside that room, those in the world whose feet were firmly planted on the ground and without a clue as to what was taking place in that room at eight o'clock every Wednesday. I asked myself, did the spirit world really exist? If so, it would appear to be separated only by certain conditions upon which it relied and through which communication was possible.

A regular communicator to the circle was a Royal Air Force boy whose mother lived only a few yards away. His mother, however, did not believe in such 'goings on' and refused an invitation to come and speak with her son. He continued to manifest in the hope that one day she might change her mind, but it was not to be. Perhaps I could sympathise with his mother's point of view in the circumstances. It must be very difficult for anyone in the outside world to accept, even remotely, the possibility of communication with anyone who has died.

One incident which I feel should be mentioned is the fact that one of the sitters, a lady, was completely deaf. The direct voice meant nothing to this lady, yet she was not left out of the proceedings. A disc-like shape materialized in front of her, the same fluorescent light shone forth from it like that of the sponge I described earlier. The difference here was that a face manifested clearly to her. The reaction was immediate and dramatic. "My God, it's him," she exclaimed. The face appeared for only a few seconds. Afterwards, she told us that it was the face of her husband and that he had died of cancer nine years before!

Apport Phenomena

A remarkable feature of Mrs Gunning's mediumship was the ability to apport objects into the room from elsewhere. A brief explanation of what this means will help the reader to appreciate the following examples.

The process, like that of all physical phenomena, is evidently governed by laws still largely unknown to science. Hence the difficulty in being able to pursue the usual methods of investigation or applying any laid down standard techniques. It is also very difficult to observe the actual process as it takes place, since the operation is carried out with great speed.

Whatever the object or matter, it is capable of being apported. Distance is of no importance. The simple theory is that the object is dematerialised in its present state, passes through space and is rematerialised through the body of the medium, emerging as a soft plastic-like replica of its original and solidifying as it drops to the floor. It is to all intents and purposes the same object which existed a few moments earlier in another part of the world, probably many miles away from where the séance is held. The objects range from small gems or precious stones to a large vase of ancient Chinese origin. Personal items which have long since been lost often turn up as a result of this kind of phenomena.

One experience I had at Mrs Gunning's séance was phenomenal, to say the least. Ivy, which had been growing on the walls outside the house, was apported into the room. It covered the floor, reaching almost up to our knees. Mrs Gunning's guide asked that the white light be switched on so that we could all see it for ourselves more clearly. As the light came on, it all dematerialised before our eyes! Presumably, it had been replaced on the walls outside. What is interesting, however, is that at the end of the séance, several insects were found crawling about the floor!

At a further séance, a profuse assortment of flowers and fruit was apported into the room. Included were bunches of black grapes, so perfect that the bloom on them was undisturbed. Some of the flowers were exotic types, completely out-of-season and not usually found in this country. In fact, the quantity was so great that it would have been impossible for anyone to have brought them into the room without being detected. The guide requested that they be distributed to sick people. My mother even arranged for some to be given to patients in the General Hospital at Southend-on-Sea. I have often wondered what those patients would have thought had they known the circumstances in which their 'gifts' were produced!

Occasionally, the sittings were not without an element reflecting the weakness of human nature. Some sitters would receive apports such as a watch or gem, but jealousy began to creep in: controversy as to 'who got what and why' resulted in a detrimental effect upon the quality of the phenomena. The guide indicated that this phase of the mediumship would cease unless the bickering stopped! As it happened, I did not experience any further apport phenomena after this absurd incident. The thought I had at the time was that it was like 'casting pearls before swine'. It seemed to me absurd that anyone could be so blind or lacking in appreciation in the face of such unique phenomena and the blessings it bestowed upon those privileged to receive it.

I have already referred to the dangers involving mediumship. The following incident illustrates clearly just how vulnerable a medium is to the wilful intervention of a sitter. At the request of one of the sitters, Mrs Gunning allowed a gentleman to attend a séance. This gentleman was a complete novice to psychic phenomena and was admitted purely on the recommendation of the sitter, who assured Mrs Gunning that he was a reliable person and would not under any circumstances step out of line or do anything that would adversely affect the séance. Half way through, he turned from his seat and switched on the white light. Anyone conversant with physical phenomena knows that white light in certain circumstances not only has a detrimental effect upon ectoplasm, in that it dissolves, but can impose a severe shock to the medium's nervous system.

In this particular instance, the medium was in the critical state of producing ectoplasm. She was covered completely with a gossamer-like material and was visible beneath it. Within a second or two of the white light being put on the substance vanished, the medium gave out a loud cry and then slumped forward in a state of collapse. The séance ended abruptly. Mrs Gunning was carried out of the room with blood streaming from her ears. It would appear that the ectoplasm was emerging from the ears at the time and the force with which it returned was so great that severe damage had been caused.

The awful stupidity, the ignorance and sheer arrogance of a sceptic attempting to 'expose' a genuine medium! Is it any wonder that such mediumship is becoming increasingly rare? Can people really complain because mediums are reluctant to expose themselves to the public at large?

Spiritualists must share some of the blame for the present dearth of physical mediumship. It is easy to cry 'Fake', 'Fraud', 'Charlatan!' This has been the signature tune of the mob for ages. Mankind has a long way to go if it is to avoid the tragedies and mistakes of the past. History continues to repeat itself with the persecution and denigration of people who are psychically gifted. At least mediums are no longer called witches and are gradually becoming recognised as responsible members of society with an important contribution to make.

I believe the future role of the medium will become as important as the physician, the scientist and even the politician. The whole philosophy of life will be looked at in a new light. Religious thinking will be streamlined and will incorporate the healing faculty together with a greater knowledge of the true nature of man and his purpose in the world. The rather fragmentary and feeble experiments now taking place in the field of ESP augur well for the future and are an attempt to focus attention on a new science which will ultimately benefit the whole human race. The need for more than material gain is apparent. What man needs is a sense of fulfilment, the exercising of his mind as well as his body and a clearer understanding of who he really is.

To live within the laws governing nature and to be in harmony with all life is a lesson which will provide man with that sense of peace and wellbeing and will reflect a changed attitude toward his fellow men for good.

Man's struggle to establish himself has only just begun. Research into the psyche and the knowledge gained will enable him to rise above the level of his material existence and view the universe in a completely new light. Life and death will take on a new meaning as man's understanding grows and his vision becomes wider. It is my opinion that this will come as a result of the development of the psychic faculties, which in turn, will increase his spiritual awareness, transcending anything that has gone before.

The last séance which I was able to attend at Mrs Gunning's house was a memorable one. For some time after the incident in which she was injured, as a result of ignorance and stupidity, the meetings were cancelled. However, later, she was able to continue on a limited scale and insisted that no guests or visitors be allowed except the regular sitters whom she could trust implicitly.

It was at this last séance that Abdul Bahá kept his promise to materialise. In fact it was one of the finest demonstrations of this phenomena that I have ever witnessed. The dignified and noble figure of Abdul Bahá materialised, surrounded in golden light. With his right hand placed on my mother's head, he pronounced a blessing upon her and then slowly dematerialised. The experience was electrifying. The presence of this man had a profound effect on everyone in that room and they had difficulty in finding words to express their thoughts. What was recognised more than anything else was the fact that they had been honoured by a true servant of God, a man of great stature, revered by millions throughout the world and recognised for his service to humanity in the cause of Unity, Peace and Brotherhood.

I often wonder what Baháis would feel if they knew that The Master, as he was called, had returned to demonstrate his survival over death. A further example of survival evidence relating to Abdul Bahá is included in a later secton dealing with Psychic Art.

Leslie Flint – Direct Voice Medium

Prior to moving to Cardiff, South Wales, I had the opportunity to attend a mass public demonstration of the independent direct voice, held at the Kingsway Hall, London. Demonstrating this type of phenomena before a large gathering in a public hall was completely new and was somewhat in the nature of an experiment. Previously, the direct voice had always been held in private circumstances with usually only a dozen or so people present. The idea on this occasion was to construct a soundproof and lightproof cabinet, placed in full view of the audience. Instead of the séance being held in total darkness, normally essential in the case of direct voice, the house lights would remain on. The medium would then be isolated in the cabinet during the meeting.

Immediately outside and in front of the cabinet, three microphones were placed to pick up the voices emanating from within the soundproof wall of the cabinet. The sound system was arranged, checked and tested by qualified technicians on the staff of the Kingsway Hall. I understood that during testing of the equipment, they had turned the amplifier up to its capacity and with a colleague inside the cabinet, shouting at the top of his voice, failed to pick up hardly a sound.

The medium for this demonstration was Mr Leslie Flint, a specialist in direct voice phenomena. The hall was packed to capacity for this first ever public demonstration. Leslie entered the cabinet, where he would remain for about the next two hours. He once told me that he suffered from claustrophobia and I can imagine that he must have found the confined space something of an ordeal.

The Chairman, the Rev C. Drayton Thomas was a man with considerable experience in physical mediumship. He gave a short talk on the *modus operandi* then handed the meeting over, as he put it, 'to the spirit world'. There was a hushed and expectant silence throughout the hall waiting for the first sign of sound through the loudspeakers. Suddenly, the first voice broke through the silence. "Cor, what a lot of people!" The voice was that of 'Mickey', Leslie Flint's spirit guide. Mickey was a London cockney newspaper boy when on earth and acted as a kind of master of ceremonies by introducing the various spirits wishing to communicate. It was obvious that Mickey was something of a comedian, for he had the audience in raptures, his humorous and down-to-earth chatter setting the scene for the first communicator.

"There is a lady here who wishes to speak to you all. She says her name is Ellen Terry." A gasp of excitement rose from the audience as a powerful voice, cultured in tone, proceeded to give a discourse about the fear of death and the philosophy of survival. My mother had known Ellen Terry, she was a well-known actress. As the voice began to speak, my mother turned to me and said "I knew that voice well, it belongs only to Ellen Terry, it's uncanny."

Several others communicated and appeared to be identified by people in the hall. The spontaneous reaction to the spirit communicators was evident by all those receiving the voice messages.

A test seance with Leslie Flint in the Kingsway Hall, London in 1946.
The cabinet with the microphone in front of it is immediately behind those seated on the raised platform.
At the table are (from left) Lord Dowding, Percy Wilson, Abdy Collins and Harold Vigurs. Noah Zerdin is at the microphone. (Photograph by permission of Psychic Press Ltd.)

However, the drama of the evening came toward the end of the séance. Mickey had been busy bringing through one person after another, enjoying the odd joke with certain members of the audience. Then he became very serious. "I have someone here now who has only been on our side of life for a few hours. He is telling me that he is the policeman who was shot last night." Murmurs rippled through the hall.

That same morning, the national press had reported the murder of a P.C. Edgar, who lived in Finchley, London. Yet here, one day later, in the Kingsway Hall, he was purporting to communicate from the spirit world. Mickey continued. "He is asking for someone named Florrie, you're up in the gallery somewhere. Will you please speak to him, it will help him get through to you." A shout from the gallery was immediate. "I'm Florrie, I'm his sister."

Only a heavy breathing at first could be heard from the loudspeakers, then a few words, gasped out in desperation. The voice was quite weak and one had to listen intently as the voice attempted to convey a message to his sister.

"The man they are looking for is in a Hastings boarding house, the gun is hidden under the mattress in his room." The policeman had great difficulty in sustaining communication and the voice faded completely. Mickey intervened to explain that a spirit which had passed only a few hours before, especially in these circumstances, needed time to adjust to the new dimension and therefore it was extremely unlikely they would be able to communicate effectively. Mickey brought the proceedings to a close because the 'power' had all been used up. He ended by telling the audience that they were responsible personally for their actions, but that redemption was open to every soul by their own efforts.

During the singing of a final hymn, two assistants entered the cabinet to help a very tired Leslie Flint from his confined space, which he had endured for the past two hours. The experiment, the first of its kind, had been a success.

The Use of Ectoplasm in Physical Mediumship

It is recognised that physical phenomena occur only through a particular kind of medium, one who has the necessary chemistry and psychic make-up for its production. Materialisation for instance, demands large quantities of ectoplasm. This is a substance produced from the medium, and other sources, in order to build up the temporary physical form of a discarnate entity. Ectoplasm is a basic raw material, used in various ways to give physical substance to a spirit manifesting through a human medium. It has the ability to mould itself into any required form or character and can be used to manipulate the various appliances in the séance room.

The colour of ectoplasm is usually white, but occasionally it is brown or black, as in the case of the materialisation of a coloured person. Ranging from the invisible to the utmost density, the texture of ectoplasm changes constantly, depending on the demands made upon it. At times, it can appear as liquid, milk-like, at the feet of the medium and rise up to solidify into a full human form in a matter of seconds. To the touch, it is slightly warm and moist, while on the other hand it can resemble the hardness of an iron bar. It has been known for it to become so hard that it is possible to drive a nail into a piece of wood with it. Yet on other occasions it appears gossamer-like and ethereal.

I have seen this substance emerge from various parts of the medium's body, ears, nostrils and the region of the solar plexus. White light appears to have a detrimental effect upon ectoplasm in that it dissolves or melts. Red light has little adverse influence and is most commonly used in the séance room[1], I am of the opinion that the question of light is not as important as Spiritualists suggest. The extent to which ectoplasm is exposed to light is dependent on the education of the medium, whose psychological fears in this respect have been handed down from the past, when physical phenomena only ever took place in complete

1. *Publisher's Note: with the intensity of the light regulated as needed.*

darkness. The old school of thought has been proved to be erroneous, since more recent phenomena have taken place in subdued white light.

That some kind of intelligence operates in the production of ectoplasm and in the manipulation of trumpets, levitation of heavy objects and the formation of human forms, capable of independent speech and thought, is quite evident. The following chapter deals with materialisation as witnessed on various occasions in good red light.

Helen Duncan – Materialisation Medium

This well-known medium was noted for her ability to produce materialisation phenomena on a scale beyond that of any other medium it has been my good fortune to observe. Up to thirty fully-formed figures would materialise at a single séance, providing evidence of their identity to those present at the séance.

During her long and successful life as a medium she was abused, denigrated, insulted and exploited. Unlike most other mediums, her séances were open to the public. The risks she took were enormous and it was inevitable that, because of this, the most outrageous atrocities were inflicted upon her. She was frequently injured and suffered ill-health as a result of wilful interference during her séances.

Mrs Duncan was a dour Scot, short in stature and stocky in build. She always insisted on two women taking her into another room in order that she could be examined before each séance. They would see her strip and put on a black dress, black knickers and a pair of black shoes (black was selected because ectoplasm is usually white and therefore stands out better against it). My friend John Kinsella and I once spoke to Mrs Duncan and she admitted that sometimes people resorted to lifting her breasts and probing the private parts of her body. I wonder what they expected to find? Her willingness to prove her genuineness and integrity was always uppermost in her mind.

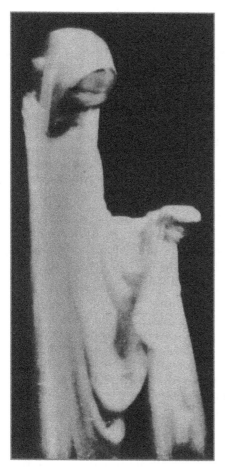

This is one of the finest photographs ever obtained of a materialisation. It was taken at a Helen Duncan séance by my late friend John Kinsella. Special permission was obtained as normally a sudden flash of white light could have serious repercussions on the nervous system of the medium.

Careful study of the photograph indicates the density and transparency of the 'ectoplasm'. The texture of this substance appears to consist of millions of minute particles suspended in space. Ectoplasm is a vibrant living substance, unlike any other material normally in existence, and is used for the temporary build-up of the physical form of a 'spirit'.

The tube-like protuberance from the side of the head is the umbilical link with the medium from whom the ectoplasm is drawn. The medium was in trance behind a black curtain.

That some would abuse their role as witnesses indicates how low they were prepared to descend in subjecting this woman to such treatment before a séance. Is it any wonder that mediums of this kind prefer to remain in obscurity and practice their gifts in private?

There was one instance, I believe, when undergoing a test séance for scientists, psychologists and researchers, she was stripped, put in a sack and told to get on with it. To the amazement of those present 'Albert', the medium's Australian Guide materialised outside the sack! It is pertinent to ask whether anyone in any other field of activity would allow themselves to be subjected to such treatment. Yet this woman was always willing to submit herself to tests and investigation in order to establish her mediumship as genuine, but most of the time all she received for her efforts was ignorant abuse and arrogant scepticism from 'experts' who understood nothing of mediumship and its complexity.

During a High Court action during the last war, Helen Duncan was prosecuted under the old Witchcraft Act. She was accused of 'pretending to conjure up spirits'! Evidence given by a policeman during the trial stated that he had attended one of her séances in plain clothes. At some stage of the proceedings he became suspicious of the phenomena and moved forward in order to secure evidence that the medium was a fraud. He grabbed at the figure which had materialised in front of the cabinet and found his arms round the medium sitting in her chair. In his evidence, he said that the figure retreated toward the rear of the cabinet as he went to grab it.

He stated that he was sure the figure was that of Mrs Duncan covered with a white sheet. When questioned as to where the white sheet had gone, since he failed to find it, he said that she must have swallowed it! A doctor, in defence, questioned the ability of anyone to swallow a sheet, particularly in the case of Mrs Duncan who, for a big woman, had a peculiarly small oesophagus. In his opinion, the idea was an impossibility – to attempt to swallow even a handkerchief would result in severe choking and asphyxia.

The absurdity of the police evidence was obvious. However, Mrs Duncan was sentenced to six months in jail. In spite of her willingness to demonstrate her mediumship before the Court, the request was refused. It was said that such a demonstration would serve no useful purpose! English justice, as I understand it, says that a person is innocent until proved guilty. Mrs Duncan's offer to prove the genuineness of her mediumship was rejected by that same Institution. Therefore, for this woman, who stood alone against the most powerful force in the land, justice was sadly lacking.

What is not generally known with regard to Helen Duncan is that at a séance in Portsmouth a sailor materialised claiming that his ship, H.M.S. Barham[2], had gone down from a torpedo fired by an enemy warship. Apart from one survivor, all personnel were lost[3]. The sailor's mother, however, was present at the séance but refused to accept that her son was dead and wrote to the Admiralty for confirmation. They communicated with her immediately, asking her where she obtained her information, as no official news had been released that the Barham had been sunk. Later, when the news was officially given out, it appeared that the ship had been sunk some weeks earlier. It is my opinion that Mrs Duncan was jailed for security reasons. The Witchcraft Act was simply a smokescreen so as not to give prominence to the fact that, through her mediumship, information of a 'secret' nature was being divulged prior to official release and that in the eyes of British Intelligence she was a menace to security!

I first met Helen Duncan in 1954 at the home of a friend in Liverpool, where she was staying for a full week. Each evening of that week she consented to give a public séance which I was privileged to attend. So, for six consecutive evenings I was able to observe very closely every aspect of the phenomena of materialisation.

Mrs Duncan's spirit guide was called Albert, when on earth, he had been a lumberjack in Australia and stood over six feet tall. At the beginning of every séance he would materialise and remain throughout, introducing the many

Publisher's Note:

2. For clarification, this séance was two years earlier in 1941/42.

3. With the present availability of information we now know although more than 850 lives were lost there were over 400 survivors of the H.M.S. Barham. We believe this may have been confused with H.M.S. Hood (only 3 survivors).

spirits wishing to communicate. The difference between Albert and his medium was well known by all who saw them together and heard them speak. Mrs Duncan had a very broad Scottish accent which I personally had a great difficulty in understanding, whereas Albert had a clear, cultured voice with an Australian accent. Mrs Duncan was a short, stout woman, while her guide was tall and lean. As Albert once remarked, "I have it one way and Mrs Duncan has it the other!"

The preliminaries were always the same as before a séance. After being stripped and searched by two ladies in another room, they would return with Mrs Duncan, testify that they were satisfied with the examination they had carried out and confirm that the medium was wearing only a pair of black knickers, a black dress and black shoes. Nothing was concealed underneath these garments.

Mrs Duncan would take her seat facing the audience and slip into deep trance very quickly. As soon as this happened the curtains, which were also black, were drawn across in front of her and the white light put out. A red light was situated directly above and in front of the 'cabinet'. A member of the audience, often about twenty in number, would lead in singing the 23rd Psalm to the tune of *Crimond*. Usually, about half-way through the second verse, a figure clothed in white would peer over the top of the curtain. Introducing himself Albert, he would ask: "Is anyone going to say 'How do you do'?" The audience would respond almost in unison "Good evening and God bless you." The séance was under way, with Albert in charge of the proceedings.

Speaking with authority and in full command Albert declared "I am going to ask Mrs Duncan to stand up now and I want you to look at the line of the face and tell me if you can see her." The audience response was unanimous. "Yes." Then, moving to the side of his medium, Albert said, "Can you see me?" "Yes," replied everyone.

There, in full view of everyone, stood both medium and guide together. Albert appeared brilliantly white against the blackness of the curtains and against Mrs Duncan, whose face alone was visible. Her dress, of course, was black, as I have previously said.

The air nearest the cabinet became distinctly chilly, a characteristic of physical phenomena. As soon as the introduction was over the guide escorted his medium back to her chair and, with a swish, pulled the curtains together. The audience sang the *Lord's Prayer* softly until Albert again addressed the audience. "The first person to come here from our side of life is a gentleman who passed as a result of a heart condition. He has only been here for a short while ... he is coming for someone sitting next to you, Alan." There was a slight pause. Continuing, Albert said, "Will that lady sitting next to Alan ask a gentleman out?"

Sitting next to me was a friend and her son, whom I had persuaded to attend in the hope that her husband would manifest. He had died in hospital only a few days previously, following an operation for a stomach ulcer. The medical staff, however, could not know that he had an abscess close to his heart! This burst and resulted in his death. This gentleman was my former boss and I knew him very well.

Slowly, the curtains parted revealing a figure smiling broadly. I recognised him immediately. Looking directly towards his wife he gasped excitedly: "Hello, darling." His son jumped up from his seat and shouted: "Skipper!" He had recognised his father. The moment was dramatic and electrifying.

His wife tried to speak but was so overcome with emotion that she found it impossible. "My dearest," said her husband, "I want you to carry on from where I left off." Then, with a wink in my direction, he said, "Thank you, Alan for your help in making this possible." He moved back a little, threw a kiss to his wife and son, and then dematerialised, seemingly through the floor!

Among the many other materialisations that evening, I must mention the mother who had lost her twin babies soon after they were born. Both materialized in the arms of Mrs Duncan, screaming their heads off! The mother went up to the cabinet and took a close look at them. From her reaction there was little doubt that they belonged to her.

Another gentleman was asked by Albert if he would like to see one of his little friends from the bottom of his garden! "Yes," he replied. Apparently he was familiar with the 'wee folk' and had seen them clairvoyantly in his garden. He even had names for each one! Albert asked Mrs Duncan to stand up and brought her forward. As she held out her arm, a tiny figure about nine inches in height materialised on her hand. A few squeaky noises issued from it as it bowed in the direction of the gentleman, who claimed he could recognise it! Spirit forms such as this are known as 'elementals' and do not have a physical existence. It is believed they play a part in the propagation of plant life. Be that as it may, the incident was interesting.

Mrs Duncan's mediumship was unique in so far as the enormous amount of ectoplasm it produced, not only to build the form but to clothe it. One evening I sat on the front row only about two feet from the cabinet and was able to gain a close look at the substance and try to formulate some clear idea as to its character and structure. Apart from the very cold air which surrounded the ectoplasm, I noticed that it gave off a strange earthy smell. It appeared to be made up of a mass of minute particles suspended in space. If one can imagine thick fog – which is a mass of tiny droplets of moisture hanging in the air – then one has some idea of its constitution. It is one of the most difficult of substances to describe since it is changing in density and fluctuating in character the whole time.

There is no doubt whatsoever that it is a living, vibrant substance. Its composition includes vital properties drawn from the medium and members of the audience, together with minute particles of dust and fibres from fabrics and the clothes worn by the people present. Mrs Gunning, the medium at Southend-on-Sea, told me on one occasion that the curtains in the séance room would, after about six months, become so threadbare that they would have to be replaced with new ones, owing to them being constantly drawn upon in the production of ectoplasm.

If the photograph on page 43, taken by my friend John Kinsella, is examined carefully, something of my description will be apparent. The edges of the ectoplasm are diffused and in some areas the substance is clearly transparent. The pipelike protrusion from the side of the head is believed to be the connecting link with the medium from which the ectoplasm emerges. When a coloured person materialised the face was black but the ectoplasmic robes with which it was clothed were white.

Mrs Duncan was a diabetic and toward the end of her active life as a medium she was again seized by a plain-clothes policeman during a séance. In a state of collapse, she was rushed to hospital. She died later[4]. The official cause of death was stated to be due to diabetes. This, of course, is a matter of opinion, since generally a person can learn to live with this condition, as Mrs Duncan did for many years.

Her death, in the circumstances, could well have been due to violation of the laws governing physical mediumship. Mrs Duncan proved to be a very resilient medium over many years. Her final séance and its consequences indicated how human she was, and that ignorant intervention at a séance, once too often, can result in dire tragedy.

The Mediumship of Alec Harris

During the course of my travels as a paint demonstrator arrangements were made for me to organise an exhibition in a large departmental store in Cardiff, South Wales. As this would last several weeks, my employer arranged for me

---

4. *Although discharged from hospital she died just six weeks later.*
(see *The Two Worlds of Helen Duncan*: G.Brealey with K. Hunter. *SNPP* 2008)

to stay at an address just outside the City with a Welsh family with whom I immediately felt at home.

The subject of psychics arose quite unexpectedly and during the conversation, it appeared that Mr Harris, the gentleman whose home I was staying at, had a brother living only a short distance away. "You should meet my brother, he dabbles in that sort of thing," said Mr Harris. I asked him his brother's name. "Alec," he said, "but don't ask me what he does, he has meetings of some kind and people come from all over the place, with their cars parked along the street." It was clear to me that he knew little of his brother's activities, and appeared to be somewhat apprehensive with respect to them.

I expressed the wish to meet Alec sometime and his brother agreed that we go round the following Sunday morning and have a chat. When we arrived, Alec was in his garden, constructing some crazy paving. His brother introduced me and after a short conversation indicating my interest and telling him of my experiences so far with psychic phenomena, he invited me to one of his healing sessions. Alec Harris was a physical medium in the same way as Mrs Gunning, of Southend-on Sea, except that his healing work was an extension of his physical mediumship.

Among the patients attending the session to which I was invited was a young man suffering with a huge carbuncle on the back of his neck. Alec placed a clean folded handkerchief over the area and proceeded to blow hard directly over the carbuncle. The act of blowing was sustained for well over a minute without pause for breath. The idea that anyone could exhale and maintain it for a period so long was, to me, a phenomenon in itself. I tried to do the same and found it to be impossible.

When the healer stopped blowing, he removed the handkerchief and to my further amazement the carbuncle had disappeared. Instead, only a deep cavity existed. The thing had literally been dematerialised! I examined the handkerchief and found it to be completely free of matter or substance. The patient, of course, was delighted. The severe throbbing pain he had been experiencing had now gone, and he said: "I felt nothing during the healing."

It occurred to me that had the patient gone to the outpatient department of a hospital to have it treated, he would not have got away with it so lightly; the lancing, the pain and so on. How lucky he was to have the benefit of a painless and speedy psychic operation without any physical discomfort whatsoever. Could this demonstrate the new medicine of the future? (See the chapter on Spiritual Healing). Several other patients, suffering from chronic conditions such as slipped disc, arthritis, sciatica, asthma and stomach ulcers, were treated and all expressed relief from the symptoms. Maybe, in spite of its modern techniques, medical practice is in some areas still clumsy compared with the healing intelligence which manifested through mediums such as Alec Harris.

As a result of further discussion, Alec invited me to his physical circle. There was no doubt in my mind that he was a medium of high calibre and I was, therefore, delighted that he should extend to me the privilege of witnessing the physical phenomena that his mediumship produced and about which he had already told me something.

On the evening of the first séance I attended at the home of Alec Harris, I first took the opportunity of discussing with members of the circle what was likely to take place. I was fascinated by what they had apparently received in the past. The phenomena appeared to differ from that of any other medium I had sat with before. No two mediums are alike. Each appears to have gifts to a greater or lesser degree; some are more developed than others, depending on the potential they possess.

Alec Harris entered the séance room wearing only a black track-suit and sat in the corner of the room between two black curtains. A dim red light was situated just above him and he was clearly visible. Within a matter of seconds from the commencement of the séance, a figure materialised and walked toward the centre of the circle. This figure was followed by another and then a third figure emerged.

The first was that of a North American Indian, sporting a magnificent headdress with feathers extending to the floor. The second was a small Chinese gentleman dressed in rich silk robes, a black hat and a pigtail which hung from the back and across one of his shoulders. The third was an Egyptian who remained close to the medium. The first two figures walked slowly round the circle so that we could observe them closely. During this time, the medium was still in his chair, head leaning to one side and obviously in a deep trance. From an occasional snore and grunt, one might easily have thought that he was simply asleep. Then something happened which I believed was hardly credible, in fact impossible.

The medium was sitting in his chair, but minus his head! The following seconds revealed that he was in the process of dematerialisation! I saw him gradually disappear until only the chair remained. Crazy? In fact impossible, but it happened. I looked around the circle to see the reaction of the other sitters and wondered if they had noticed this extraordinary incident. Unable to resist any longer, I queried what I believed had happened, just in case it could have been an hallucination! An immediate response came from the medium's wife. "Oh, it's alright," she said, "He will be somewhere around, they often take him away." At this, the North American Indian assured everyone that the medium was alright and would return shortly.

Later, the Indian turned to the medium's wife and said, "I want you to unlock the door, go downstairs and into the garden. There you will find your husband on his knees. Wake him up and bring him back to the séance room!" She promptly obeyed the instruction and returned with Alec who calmly took his seat and 'slipped' into trance again. The three materialisations had, through all this, remained and held conversations with the sitters! Then, almost without warning, each began to dematerialise. The Egyptian first, and then the Chinese figure. The Indian walked over to the medium's wife and taking one of the largest feathers from his headdress, he handed it to her. "I would like you to have this," he said, "to keep, in memory of my visit." He then dematerialised.

Direct voice was manifested to most of the sitters, as well as apport phenomena.

The experiences of that evening were remarkable and must raise a lot of questions and doubts in the minds of anyone not fortunate to experience such phenomena. It is understandable that they find it difficult to accept. Verbal descriptions cannot hope to match personal experience and though most of my friends do accept many of the things I have told them, I do not ask or expect them to believe me, because it was not their experience. All I could do was to explain what I had seen with my normal senses of intelligence, reason, vision and hearing. If these are reliable in every-day life, why should they differ in the séance room?

Conjurors, magicians and psychologists all attempt to explain away these phenomena as hallucination, collective hypnosis or other such unlikely alternatives, rather than admit that they do not understand them because they are outside their normal experience. Were they a little more tolerant, they might even learn a little concerning these apparent mysteries. There may well be alternative explanations for the phenomena from that of the Spiritualist hypothesis, but until more is known and understood in relation to the forces and nature underlying the phenomena, I do not believe anyone is in a position to be dogmatic.

My purpose is to describe the phenomena I have witnessed, not to explain it, which is quite a different thing. Perhaps the reader will gain something from my personal views. These are put forward in the final chapters of the book.

The Mediumship of William Olsen

Another physical medium with whom I had the pleasure of sitting on several occasions was William Olsen. Mr Olsen, of Sheerness, was a placid, unpretentious person who always gave me the impression that he was completely bored with the whole thing, especially just prior to giving a séance. I remember watching him being tied to his chair by two of the sitters and thinking how ordinary he looked. There was no slick or devious manner displayed as with stage performers, he was simply a quiet, unsophisticated character with little trace of ego or self-importance. As a medium, his demonstration might not put him in the higher grade, but he appeared to be an honest man, sincere in his own peculiar way. I always believed that his mediumship was capable of greater things but it appeared that somewhere along the line, the development had stopped short and failed to progress any further. However, the phenomena he did produce left me in no doubt that his mediumship was genuine.

Many would question the purpose of his mediumship and whether or not it provided sufficient evidence for survival. Whatever the case, one was forced to recognise that some powerful force was at work, even though to some people, it was not of a highly intelligent nature. One communication through the direct voice was most interesting and involved myself, with my wife sitting at the other end of the room. I will refer to this later.

Much of the routine of an Olsen séance was repetitive. This, in some respects was an advantage so far as scientific investigation is concerned, as scientists prefer to study something that can be reliably repeated. For instance, the supernormal removal of the medium's jacket, although it was stitched right up the front with the ropes tightly securing the medium's arms and legs to his chair. The fantastic levitation of the trumpets and their consequent performance; these alone, and in themselves, were sufficient for anyone to be amazed.

The only item of equipment that Mr Olsen used which was not employed by other mediums I had sat with was a rheostat lamp attached to his chair. This was controlled during the séance by the guide in charge of the proceedings. The intensity of the lamp could be adjusted at any given moment according to the requirements and phase of phenomena demonstrated. Mr Olsen did not use a cabinet or sit behind curtains as other mediums had done. He would form part of a large circle, about twenty in number, and request that each sitter be linked to the next by elastic bands around their wrists, as part of his precautions against anyone leaving their seat during the séance. It would be difficult for anyone attempting to do so without the person sitting next to them knowing about it.

The séances I attended were all very noisy affairs and at times, almost amounted to bedlam. From the moment the white light was put off, things began to happen. The two trumpets on the floor would rise and gyrate around the room in opposite directions. They would gather speed and momentum with each second in flight. Then the remainder of the paraphernalia, a tambourine, mouth organ and drum —complete with sticks – would take off and join forces with the two trumpets. While this was happening, various sitters were shrieking at the top of their voices. I think they believed that they had to do this to keep the 'vibrations' up. It is an old school of thought among Spiritualists that the more noise the sitters can make, the better the results. I never found this to be the case. Everything is dependent upon the quality of the medium's development. This, in my opinion, is the only criteria in the production of good physical phenomena.

What with the noise, the singing and everything whirling around the room, the atmosphere was a mixture of amusement and pandemonium. Suddenly, everything would crash to the floor as if the power had been withdrawn. For a moment, all activity would cease, but only for a moment. A trumpet would levitate slowly and move over to one of the sitters opposite me. As it happened, it was hovering in front of my wife's face. A voice, with a Welsh accent, issued forth, "We are very sorry about the baby, but never mind, two good halves make a whole." As this statement was being made, the trumpet moved swiftly back and forth between my wife and myself sitting directly opposite her. There was no breaking the continuity of the speech and it was remarkable in the way it linked us both together. My wife's family are Welsh and we had recently lost our baby. No one in that room but us knew about this, least of all the medium.

After various other communications with the sitters, the guide would intervene to suggest that they try and remove the medium's coat. (see illustration opposite). He requested that everyone sing quietly while they were preparing things behind the scenes. During the singing, the guide increased the intensity of the rheostat lamp in order that everyone would be able to see the demonstration clearly. The phenomena commenced with the emergence of a white mass of ectoplasm which built up on the front of the medium's coat. Gradually it elongated to form an arm-like structure with finger-like protuberances. These were used to manipulate the coat which was lifted completely above the medium's head and thrown forward to the floor. The medium was now in his shirt sleeves, with the ropes still secure and binding his arms to the chair practically undisturbed.

I leave the reader to think about this very carefully. They would find it impossible to remove a jacket in the same circumstances. The jacket was buttoned and stitched from top to bottom and the arms were securely bound with the sleeves under the ropes. Every stage of the phenomena was visible to all the sitters in the room.

Note: While it was not possible to obtain a picture of Mr Olsen's coat being removed the reader can see the illustration reproduced by kind permission of Harry Edwards from his book, The Mediumship of Jack Webber. *Jack Webber was a more advanced medium than William Olsen, but the illustration shows something of the kind of phenomena involving the medium's coat.*

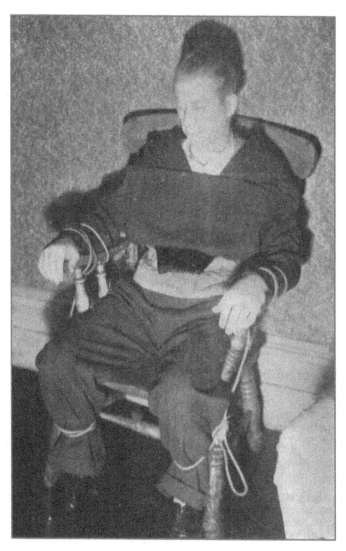

Phenomenal manipulation of the medium's coat.

(medium Jack Webber) - photo by HarryEdwards who took the photo himself with infra-red light showing a remarkable stage in the removal of the coatby supernormal means. Careful study of the picture shows parts of the coat in positions which would normally be impossible to reproduce. Note the back of the coat and the collar at the front of the medium.

(Photo from *The Mediumship of Jack Webber,* by Harry Edwards)

The climax of an Olsen séance was the complete levitation of the medium in his chair whilst securely bound to it. He would be taken up toward the ceiling, round the room and then he would gently float to the floor again. Whatever one might say about such a performance, and there were many who were dubious of his mediumship, Mr Olsen left me in no doubt whatsoever that his mediumship was above reproach. If a conjuror or magician were to reproduce the same effects, a lorry load of props and electronic equipment would be necessary as well as an army of people to set up the props and operate the electronic equipment. A good physical medium requires no props.

I wonder how far any of those who suggest fraud would get in the same circumstances in which a medium is prepared to sit? No one, to my knowledge, ever proved fraud against any of the mediums I have so far described, including Mr William Olsen.

The Angel of Bersham

The Angel of Bersham was the term given to Sister Helen, Guide of Mrs Richards, a lesser known physical medium but nonetheless exceptional Mrs Richards was known as 'Floss' to her sitters. The circle took place in her home in Bersham, North Wales. I was privileged to sit with her on odd occasions as did Mr D.H. Shaw, the Manchester physical medium. Floss had a nun guide who materialised and often invited mothers in the locality to bring their newly born children to be 'Christened' by her. On returning the child to the mother she would dematerialise.

Sister Helen, as she was known, was a beautiful soul. Floss's mediumship was reported by *Psychic News* after its Editor, at that time, Maurice Barbanell visited the circle and witnessed for himself the astounding phenomena, when three materialisations would appear at the same time. I recall one occasion in a private house with a huge coal fire burning, when 'Sister Helen' controlled her medium then walked over to the fire and calmly took a large red hot lump of coal out of the grate with her bare hands and took it over to her seat and placed it upon her head. Not a single hair was singed. The coal was later placed back on the fire with no harm to the medium. A perfect example how the Spirit Guides can render the human body immune to the effects of burning coal when placed on the body, as was demonstrated in this instance.

Psychic Photography

What are known as 'psychic extras' and which appear on a photograph when taken by certain people, have, in the past, produced some extraordinary results. At the same time, psychic photography has come under fire from the sceptics for many years. Experiments carried out to produce this type of phenomena have certainly proved to me that activity of a supernormal kind can be reproduced in the form of images/rods (visible manifestation of unorganised psychic energy), and even faces of people who have passed away. I am not in a position to argue the case for or against pioneers in this field who are no longer with us, but I am in possession of a number of psychic photos depicting dead relatives. The medium responsible for literally thousands of such photographs was a gentleman named William Hope.

Mr. Hope lived in Crewe and was an amateur photographer who began by taking photographs of weddings[5]. For some time, he was disturbed at the

5. *Publisher's Note:*
William Hope's beginnings in Psychic photography have been recorded as follows: he took a picture of a workmate one Saturday which when developed showed the figure of the man's dead sister alongside him. He took a second one and this time the baby was with her. A colleague recognised it as a 'spirit photo'. In Crewe he met Mr & Mrs Buxton at the Spiritualist church and they formed a circle for his development. This does not mean that he did not have 'extras' on wedding photos and the Author may have been told this by Mrs Hughes who gave the Author the photographs. (See Rev C. Tweedale: News from the Next World. Psychic Book Club 1947 & A. Conan Doyle The Case for Spirit Photography. Hutchinson & Co c.1924)

appearance of white blobs and faces of people who were not supposed to be there. It was only when certain members of the wedding groups recognised the faces as those of relatives who had passed on, that he learned of his own 'powers' in this respect. As the 'gift' developed, he became more and more popular until the demand for sittings, especially from the bereaved, was enormous. The question is: do the faces of dead people appearing on a photographic plate or film, taken by a person who has never met the sitter before and knows nothing whatsoever about them, constitute evidence of survival, especially when those faces are clearly recognised by those attending the sitting?

The illustrations included in this book were passed to me by a lady who knew William Hope very well. The photographs were taken by him in her home. Some in the conservatory outside in bright sunlight! I accept them as genuine simply because I believe in the honesty and sincerity of the person, who was a gifted medium in her own right. She had received excellent evidence herself and testifies to the integrity of William Hope, according him the recognition she felt he deserved for his mediumship. Many well-known researchers visited him and were impressed by the results which were achieved.

I should point out that some critics, and professional photographers in particular, are unable to understand why the light falls differently on the subject sitting for the photograph from the resultant 'extra'. Normally this would indicate that the extra had been superimposed, since the two were not taken at the same time. There is in fact a form of superimposition in that the extra, not being visible at the time of exposure is imprinted by effecting a chemical change upon the film's emulsion surface by supernormal means.

Apart from the above point, only the evidence can decide whether this is achieved by supernormal or fraudulent means.

Uri Geller demonstrated that his own image could appear on photographic film in the camera while the cap remained over the lens! If neither the film nor the subject was exposed to light, how was it possible for an image to appear at all?

This same question applies to psychic photography in a similar way. As with most psychic phenomena, energy of some form is employed and intelligently directed to produce results contrary to what is normally possible and beyond the laws at present known to science. The energy, which is directed by the mind, is able to influence matter. The mind could be incarnate or discarnate. It is my opinion that both the living and the influence of the 'dead' can produce the phenomena. The results present a challenge that cannot be ignored if the problems they pose are to be solved or understood in their true context.

This photograph is of a lady named Mrs Davies, from Liverpool. She was ill at the time of the sitting but did not want to miss the opportunity. She remarked at the time, "I don't know who will come, for I have had them all." When she saw the picture she laughed and shouted, "It's Jimmy." This was a boy who used to shout through her letter-box, "Spirits, spirits". He died in the First World War.

Mrs Davies herself was a powerful medium, which could account for the very unusual 'extra'.

The photograph above is of a gentleman also from Liverpool and shows a fine 'spirit extra' of his father. Note the likeness in the features.

All the 'spirit' photographs on these pages were taken on glass-plates by Mr William Hope, a gifted psychic photgraphic medium.

This picture has an unusual story. The young man was an atheist and only decided to sit out of curiosity. When he saw the photograph he thought someone had obtained a copy of his father's picture, missing from the family album and was convinced it was a fraud. Later his wife told him that she had sent the photograph to his brother in America six months earlier.

This lady was a member of a local Spiritualist church. The 'extra' is a clear picture of her brother, who died some years earlier. Again note the likeness of the features.

This group sat and were surprised to see the appearance of a nun. The lady on the extreme left claimed that the 'extra' was her spirit guide. Note the clever way in which the black curtain in the background has been used to show the nun's habit. This picture was taken in a conservatory (lean-to) in bright sunlight.

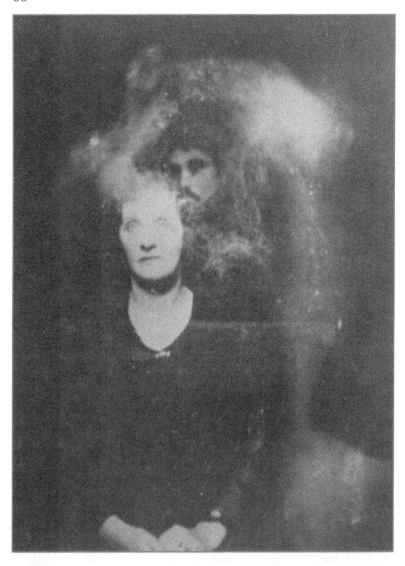

This lady sat for the photograph only three days after the death of her husband. She was in mourning. Her husband is clearly visible behind his wife's head.

An early photograph illustrating the way psychic energy is used in table phenomena. Note the hand manifesting beneath the table and the way the energy appears to emerge from the sitter on the extreme right of the photograph.

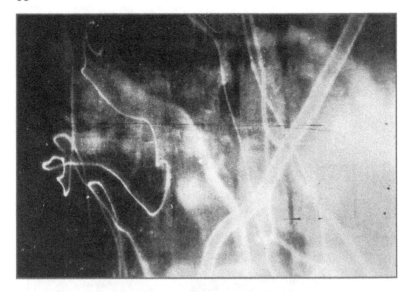

This photograph shows 'unorganised' psychic energy commonly known as 'psychic rods'. Note the varying characteristics of the rods. Results like this often appear in early attempts at developing this type of mediumship. Complete features come when the mediumship is fully developed. (Experimental photograph taken by the author.)

Psychic Art

This aspect of mediumship is generally dependent upon the medium possessing the clairvoyant faculty in addition to the ability to paint or draw what they 'see'. A striking example of psychic art is illustrated overleaf. Here, you see a photograph of Abdul Bahá, the distinguished Leader of the Bahá'í Religion, taken during his earthly life, together with that of a painting done by a psychic artist many years after his passing.

To appreciate the value of this kind of evidence, it is better that a medium completely unknown to the sitter is selected and vice-versa so that what is produced by the psychic artist is likely to be more evidential. The portrait of Abdul Bahá was painted by a woman medium from London. My mother arranged the sitting in the usual way. Neither knew the other and had never before met.

At the sitting, the medium did a quick portrait of her mother, but before it was completed, she put it to one side and said, "Your mother insists that I leave her portrait and instead, paint one of an eastern gentleman who is here, that you knew some years ago. She says that his name is Abdul." The completed picture was without doubt that of Abdul Bahá. The reader can judge the accuracy and likeness between the photograph and the psychic drawing.

My mother joined the Bahá'í Movement in Manchester about 1922. At that time, a call went out from Abdul Bahá in Haifa, to Bahá'ís throughout the world to contribute toward the building of a huge temple at Wilmette, on the shore of Lake Michigan, U.S.A. Having little means at the time, my mother was unable to make a contribution in the usual way. She did, however, have long red hair, for which Hollywood were offering eleven guineas an ounce. She decided to sell it, the proceeds from which she would give as her contribution toward the building of the temple.

A Persian Bahá'í finally bought the hair and was so impressed by my mother's act, that he wrote to Abdul Bahá in Palestine, seeking permission for the hair to be displayed in the temple, upon its completion. Abdul Bahá at once wrote to my mother. The letter was written in Arabic and had to be translated at Balliol College, Oxford. In the letter, Abdul Bahá declared that had he known the sacrifice she was to make in the Bahá'í Cause, he would have contributed on her behalf. The incident and full text of the letter is published in early Bahá'í literature.

Another technique employed in the field of psychic art is where the medium purports to be 'controlled' by a spirit guide who, when on earth, was an artist. It is my experience that this type of medium seldom provides satisfactory evidence, other than to produce an enormous number of portraits of spirit guides. This may give some comfort to some people. But it is extremely difficult to obtain evidence of identity of a guide because one invariably has nothing with which to compare it, such as a photograph or a previous portrait done independently by another artist. I know of people with lots of pictures of guides yet long for one depicting a relative or loved one they can recognise! It would appear that a good psychic artist is equally as rare as a good physical medium.

Psychic painting of
Abdul Bahá

A photograph of him
for comparison

The above example illustrates dramatically the kind of 'evidence' which can be obtained through a psychic artist. The medium 'sees' clairvoyantly the person who wishes to communicate and transfers this to the canvas or paper. Evidence which can be compared with a photograph provides the sitter with a visual record of the person who appears to the medium.

Chapter 3

Clairvoyance and Precognition

The faculties of clairvoyance and precognition are closely allied. They demonstrate the ability of some people to go forward or backwards in time. In the case of clairvoyance, the medium 'sees' with the psychic vision and obtains information through the psychic senses. This is interpreted with descriptions of people, places or events past, present and future. It could be said that clairvoyance, when accompanied by evidence regarding those who have passed, is a means of communicating with the spirit world.

On the other hand, there are clairvoyants who specialise. They concentrate on finding missing people and often provide valuable information regarding murder cases. The same faculty is used to help people whose domestic and business life is confused and who need some guidance as to the future. So it is with the personal and marital situations of a person's life. They often seek help from a clairvoyant who may be able to 'see' round the corner and offer a solution to a particular problem. A good fortune teller employs a certain amount of clairvoyance combined with intuition and psychology – plus a measure of guesswork?

Up to now, I have avoided any reference to my own psychic faculties which were developed to a degree over a period of about ten years. This was acquired through deliberate and disciplined methods with the aid of competent guidance. Above all, the development was pursued with intention and purpose until the time arrived when it was possible to demonstrate publicly, both clairvoyance and trance mediumship. The trance mediumship provided in the main, spiritual philosophy concerning healing, psychic development and a general pattern for improved living. Extracts from some of the talks given whilst in trance are included in the chapters on healing and psychic development. They will indicate to the reader something of the nature of the kind of philosophy issued through a trance medium in relation to various subjects and the contribution they make to a better understanding of those subjects.

Clairvoyance comes in the category of mental mediumship involving the interpretation of images and symbols. These, [in my case], are received in the form of pictures which move across the mind's eye like a kind of ticker-tape. The information often comes in short bursts with a spontaneity that is characteristic. One soon learns to differentiate between conjured-up thoughts or imagination during development. In any case, the evidence of this is reflected in the results obtained. Again, as I have often stated, the test of any mediumship is dependent upon the evidence it provides and no amount of irrelevant jargon can substitute for this.

Evidence that can be corroborated is the ultimate basis upon whether or not the medium is genuine or merely fishing, padding, or even guessing. If a medium claims to be psychic, then he should deliver the goods the same way as a musician, artist or engineer is expected to do in their capacity or profession. If he is unable to demonstrate competently, then he should go back to school and continue with his lessons!

Development of the psychic faculties is a continuing process and no one can claim that they are fully developed. Like the acquisition of knowledge, it is constantly necessary to maintain progress and advance in understanding of the many new revelations man is subject to in his evolvement. An open mind is a receptive mind.

Some Examples of Clairvoyance
(demonstrated by the Author)

The following examples of clairvoyance illustrate how, as a result of developing the psychic senses, one is able to obtain information that is not normally available by the usual means of communication. The question arises as to whether such information can be regarded as evidence of contact with the spirit world or if some other explanation accounts for the information received and transmitted by the medium. The examples selected were given in public halls at different times. With the exception of one recipient, the persons involved were completely unknown to me.

Example No.1

Pointing to a lady in the audience, I proceeded to give a message as follows: "I am getting with you the name of a person called DELAMEY, linked with a place called BELAMERE. This person passed away in some kind of institution as a result of a lung condition." I then asked the recipient if they could place the message. The recipient replied, "The name wasn't DELAMEY, it was BELLAMY, he died from pneumonia in a sanatorium in DELAMERE. He was my husband."

Example No.2

Another case of a lady sitting at the back of the hall: "I have a gentleman here in Officer's uniform but this man had no sense of smell." Immediately, the recipient responded "That's right. He is my Major, my husband. You are right, he had no sense of smell."

Example No.3

This time, to a lady in the front row of the hall.

"With you, I have seen a dorothy bag with a piece of coal inside it. Do you know what this could mean?"

The recipient replied, "Well, my name is Dorothy and my husband, who has passed on, was a coalman." "That may be so," I said, "but to me, the bag and the coal indicate that you will be coming into some money. Will you watch for it in the next few days?" Exactly one week later, this lady won some money from a crossword puzzle! She told me that she was a pensioner and the money was greatly appreciated.

Example No.4

This last example involved a friend whom I knew fairly well, although I tried to avoid such people at demonstrations for obvious reasons. Here was a clear case where information came that was not known to the medium, yet provided evidence of my friend's son who had been killed in Holland during the last war. I already knew of this and the name of the son. However, let the message speak for itself.

Pointing to my friend, I said, "I do know you, but I have to say there is someone here referring to some pearl beads, they are talking about a girl named Kathy. Does it mean anything to you?" "Yes," she replied, "My son wrote to me from Holland during the war and asked me to purchase some pearl beads for his fiancée, her name was Kathy. My son was killed shortly after writing the letter. However, I bought the beads and sent them on to Kathy."

Clairvoyance of this nature can mean one of two things. Either the information is being communicated by a spirit, or the medium is unconsciously picking up the information telepathically from the recipient. ESP experiments support this view of telepathic communication between medium and recipient. In my opinion, I do not think anyone can be dogmatic as to the true source of such information. Whether it is from the living or the dead or both, is something that science may be able to provide the answer to once it decides to investigate the matter seriously. Until this happens, I believe one is entitled to consider the Spiritualist hypothesis as having some relevance. After all, in the absence of proof, the evidence is strongly in favour of survival.

Precognition

Precognition is the ability to 'see' events before they occur. I believe this faculty is a by-product of clairvoyance, in which the medium is able to go forward or backwards in time, describing people, place and events. Again, I intend only to give personal evidence of precognition and leave the reader to think about it in the light of the whole range of supernormal phenomena. The evidence for precognition is overwhelming. I wonder how many lives could be saved by heeding the warnings given by those who have this faculty?

Example No.1

In 1968, I visited the home of a friend. During the evening, I suddenly 'saw' the map of Scotland, then Glasgow appeared in large letters. This was replaced with a series of pictures depicting buildings collapsing and general chaos. I felt it was some kind of earthquake. I was impelled to speak about this and added that I felt there was going to be a disaster in Scotland, Glasgow in particular.

The following morning, all the national newspapers reported a violent hurricane which had hit Glasgow during the night. Hundreds of buildings were either damaged or had collapsed with loss of life. Approximately six hours separated the time of the precognition and the event taking place. But would anyone in authority have taken notice of such a warning based on the exercise of ESP? Maybe in the future, such a basis will be regarded with the seriousness it deserves. Perhaps, it will become commonplace to act on the warnings and advice of suitably gifted people who gain information through tried and tested sources of psychic origin. It would be one way of using psychic energy for the positive good and protection of the community.

Example No.2

On Saturday evening at about 11pm. on 18th October, 1957, I had reason, psychically, to believe that my father had died in London, some 225 miles away from where I was living in Liverpool. The evening before, I had sent my sister to London on the strength of a clairvoyant vision that he was wandering about the streets of London in a delirious state. My sister first went to Southend in Essex, where my father lived. When she arrived, my mother informed her that Dad had left home two weeks earlier and that she had no idea of his whereabouts. She then travelled to London and scoured almost every hospital in London in case he had been admitted to one of them. Finally almost exhausted, she stood on the steps of the London Hospital, despondent and undecided as to whether to enquire, she came away and caught the midnight train home to Liverpool. She arrived back early on Sunday morning and told me her story. I told her that I feared Dad was dead and that it was only a question of time before we knew officially. However, the following morning, Monday, I received a card from my mother. It stated, "Dad died in the London Hospital on Saturday evening about 11pm., letter following. Love, Mother." The letter which followed confirmed that my father had been found wandering about London and was a very sick man. He was taken to a Salvation Army hostel where he collapsed and was then taken to the London Hospital.

The experience illustrates that the development of the psychic faculty makes one acutely aware of impending dangers or tragedies as well as the more pleasant events, one of which follows in the next example.

Example No.3

A young man gave me his watch to psychometrise. The first thing I 'saw' was him waving a conductor's baton. I told him that he would take part in a contest where musical skill was involved. Also, he would be engaged in teaching young people.

Some time later, he was invited to captain a team on the B.B.C. T.V. programme, *Top of the Form*, where his team was successful in providing correct answers to some difficult questions on music. I learned too, that he had accepted, against his will, an appointment as a teacher and was now confronting young people in this capacity.

Example No.4

The final example relates to my sister, Eileen, whom I had sent to London to enquire about my father. Eileen later married an American and had gone to live in Australia. One day, I turned to my wife and said, "We are going to lose Eileen. In twelve months she will be dead." I was stunned at such a possibility and tried to dismiss it from my mind, but I knew it was going to happen. I wrote to my sister several times enquiring as to how she was getting on. Her letters were vague and finally she stopped writing. I wrote again and again, but still no reply came from her.

Exactly twelve months to the day of my precognition, I received an airmail letter from a neighbour in Australia to tell me that Eileen was found dead in bed. She had two nice boys. The reasons for her death are too personal to relate here.

During the time I practised as a medium, I was asked on several occasions to psychometrise a personal item such as a ring or a watch. Psychometry is the practice of holding an object and 'reading' the psychometric vibrations which emanate from it. These vibrations are interpreted, providing information concerning the owner of the object and associations with their personal life. Valuable information can be obtained through this method of divination regarding murder cases and missing persons, providing of course, that the object has some close link with the person involved.

Ghosts, Poltergeists and Hauntings

Volumes have already been written in regard to this aspect of psychic activity. Therefore I do not propose to deal with the subject at length. Much of the evidence put forward is undoubtedly coloured and dramatised for various reasons such as commercialism, sensationalism and probably as a result of pure gullibility. Actual cases of this type of manifestation are rare, but when they do occur, are very real, especially to those fortunate or unfortunate enough to witness them! To define the nature of ghosts, for instance, or the phenomena attributed to them is to stick one's neck out! Therefore, any attempt to explain these phenomena is done so with the utmost reservation. My opinion is speculative because I do not claim, by any means, to know all the answers.

The vague and ethereal manifestations we call ghosts could be described as 'thought forms' emanating from the living and manifesting as external entities. These residual thought forms may have their associations with the past lives of people who once lived in the body, as well as incarnate beings. Objects, buildings and places all record something of the personality of those having been associated with them, depending upon the intensity of that association. A ghost can be simply the temporary revitalisation of a memory from the past, like an echo or remnant. This dormant fragment is infused with psychic energy flowing from the living and has no intelligence of itself.

A ghost has never been known to harm anyone physically, except to introduce a state of fear, particularly when one experiences something that is inexplicable. Most of the phenomena concerning 'ghosts' can, in my opinion, be attributed to emanations from the living and is the result of a distorted release of psychic energy, influenced by the subconscious mind.

Poltergeists, on the other hand, present a different picture inasmuch as they are reputed to produce boisterous effects such as the throwing of objects, causing mysterious fires and generally creating a disturbance. The question often asked is whether spirits, malicious or evil, are responsible for this kind of phenomena. I venture to suggest, like that of ghosts, the energy behind the phenomena emanates from human beings in the vicinity of the occurrences, but the intelligence has its source in the subconscious mind of the individual.

I think it is agreed that we are all capable of malicious acts of violence. Only the fact that the majority of us have disciplined ourselves from resorting to such behaviour saves us from acting consciously in this direction. However, the subconscious probabilities and urges may find expression through the psychic self, so that what I am suggesting is that poltergeist phenomena could well be the result of releasing an excess of this energy which then manifests as an external act of vandalism, the intelligence having its source in the subconscious mind. The physical phenomena of telekinesis often lack purpose and are so unorganised because the psychic energy is neither channelled nor under specific control as it would be in the conditions of the séance room.

As I have indicated already, all psychic phenomena rely upon energy. If that energy is not controlled, then variations and distortions are likely to occur, hence the pointless manifestations that could include poltergeists among them. It is believed that adolescents have an excess of unchallenged psychic energy and periodically, this builds up, is released and results in the happenings I have described. Unlike developed mediums, the manifestations point to undeveloped potential simply requiring direction and correct channelling.

Exorcism

This form of ritual or invocation to dispel or remove a spirit has been pursued by the Church for centuries. Whether it is a valid method of getting rid of spirits is open to question. For one thing, how many clergymen are qualified either in psychic knowledge or understanding to deal with cases of hauntings and poltergeists?

The assumption that all activity of a psychic nature is due to evil spirits may well be erroneous. There are many instances of psychic disturbances where exorcism is futile and serves only to increase the phenomena. In the case of a spirit whose motive for manifesting is to try and communicate something of vital importance, it is sheer arrogance on the part of 'experts' to assume them to be evil. No doubt the resentment felt by the spirit at anyone trying to give them the 'brush off' or evict them would, in my opinion, only make them more determined to stay put! We preach tolerance and freedom for the living, why not the same democratic right for a spirit to go or stay where it pleases?

I suspect that we have far more to fear from the living than the 'dead' and what is required in a number of cases of hauntings and other psychic disturbances is a closer investigation of the mental stability of those who claim to be the victims of such phenomena. It would be nearer the truth to suggest that many people need a psychiatrist rather than a priest!

Again, it is more than likely that if spirits are about a particular place and continue to go about their business, they are quite oblivious of the living, simply because of the dimension in which they exist. To attribute blame for psychic activity to them is to shift the responsibility from where it truly lies – with the living and the complex nature of their own psychic potential.

Trance Mediumship

The question of the trance state, through which spirit guides purport to control the medium for the purpose of delivering philosophy, communicating information and diagnosing illness continues to present a problem as to whether they are a product of the subconscious mind, secondary personalities or the result of independent sources, e.g. discarnate entities in their own right. Very rarely does the evidence suggest the latter to be the case. Many years of experience observing mediums in the trance state has led me to believe that only in extremely isolated instances, where the evidence cannot be easily explained away, is there justification for accepting the separate entity theory. There is no doubt that many of the guides which manifest through entranced mediums utter some extraordinary and profound philosophy as well as verbiage. It has been suggested very often that guides are the product of the subliminal self where the super-conscious faculty of the individual is able to express itself.

The trance state is self-induced. This can be achieved with practice. Once the temporary suspension of consciousness exists, the way is then open for the subconscious mind to come into play and this is where a great deal of confusion arises.

Spiritualists have a tendency to attribute most if not all activity manifesting through an entranced medium to discarnate sources, without taking into consideration the innate potential of the medium and the ability to produce the phenomenon which is invariably within the possibility of the medium's intelligence and capacity. The potential of an incarnate being should not be underestimated when deciding whether or not one 'intelligence' is at work as opposed to another, for both are intelligent.

While there are many cases of trance mediumship being genuine and providing room for thought, the dividing line is very thin and lends substance to the charge that in a number of instances the medium is simply dramatising deep-rooted thoughts arising from the subconscious mind. There may be a deliberate intention to display or act out a preconceived set of ideas. This comes in the category of conscious fraud.

On the other hand, the probability of subconscious fraud cannot be ruled out either. This is where the medium has no conscious control, but the subconscious intelligence is operative. In this case there is no deliberate intention on the part of the medium to perpetrate fraud, but they can, in fact, become a victim of their own unconscious state. A large part of the phenomena of the séance room could well be explained in this way, whether it is physical or mental.

The difficulty at the present stage of our knowledge, in regard to this subject, is how one discriminates between subconscious activity of the medium and the intervention of a discarnate influence or entity. Generally a discarnate entity is expected to display super intelligence and possess knowledge far in advance of our own, why this should be so is difficult to understand, since with the majority of trance mediums the substance that manifests falls far short of this standard and in some cases does not match the normal intelligence of the medium through whom it manifests.

That some trance mediums exhibit spasmodic and fragmentary moments of illumined philosophy or snatches of brilliant clairvoyance, may not be due to the trance state itself and the spirit which purports to be in control, but simply an expression of their own 'super-conscious level'. In any case, the best clairvoyance is often demonstrated by mediums in full control of their minds without resorting to trance or self-hypnosis. Likewise, some of the best speakers talk more sense in their conscious state than many who allow themselves to be used in the trance state.

I have suspected for some time that a psychological explanation lies behind the problem of trance mediumship in general. Some of the finest mediums I have known, whether they are healers, clairvoyants or physical mediums find it unnecessary to use the trance condition when demonstrating mediumship. They prefer to rely on attunement with the 'powers that be', whilst retaining their own normal mental state. This method surely indicates a far greater degree of development and is probably the reason why it is often more convincing and evidential. There is no shifting of responsibility to some abstract source or the need to hide behind closed eyelids. The medium is personally responsible for what happens since he is able to exercise his free will at any time. Therefore, it is the medium in the final analysis who calls the tune. No guide or spirit can use him against his will and without his knowledge neither does he allow the trance state to take place unless he himself decides to induce it!

Frequent exhibitions in developing circles are, in my opinion, responsible for the poor standard of many trance mediums who leave the developing circle having had little or no competent guidance from the leader of such a group. The lack of discipline and knowledge simply produces a pseudo-trance or 'shut-eye' performance which is all too common among many members of developing circles.

The leaders of such groups do nothing to discourage this kind of behaviour, either because of ignorance or possibly a vested interest in-so-far that it is better to have a bunch of gullible fools to furnish the collection plate than none at all! I have seen so many instances of people deluded by the antics and callisthenics of pseudo-trance that it is no wonder those in the rational world outside tend to regard some Spiritualists with a mixture of sympathy and amusement!

I remember one lady sitting in a development group rising up from her seat after a period of puffing and blowing, put her hand above her eyes as though looking far into the distance. The other members of the group turned toward her with outstretched hands in order to give more 'power'. Then, in an assumed deep voice, she declared, "Hi am Herr Von Ribbentrop, Hi am looking for my harmy." (No, there is not a mistake in the spelling). As an observer, I pointed out to this lady afterwards that Herr Von Ribbentrop was the German Foreign Minister and did not possess an army! All I received from her was abuse!

Ignorance on this level is a common feature. Another case was that of a woman who believed she was controlled by a pet dog she had lost some years previously. Crawling about the floor on all fours, she proceeded to bark. Several in the group muttered, "God bless you friend"!

So far as trance mediumship is concerned, it can afford a vehicle for discarnate agencies to manifest, but can also allow the super-consciousness to reveal aspects of knowledge that do not find normal expression through the conscious mind. Extracts from a booklet compiled from tape recordings of talks given in trance by my spirit guide, 'White Eagle', are reproduced in this book to illustrate something of the philosophy and guidance offered through a developed trance medium. I have included them because I feel they contribute toward a better understanding of the complexities of mediumship and their implications.

At the same time, I reserve judgment as to the real source of these talks and do not fully accept that they are the result of a discarnate entity, which so many people came to know and love, as White Eagle. What I do feel, however, is that we have a great deal to learn and understand as to the real nature and the mechanics of the mental processes involved. It has been suggested that it doesn't matter really where the information comes from – that it serves to improve our knowledge is the important thing, especially regarding our purpose for being here and where possibly we may be going.

Uri Geller -The Mind Bender

This young Israeli presented the scientific world with their greatest challenge so far regarding the forces behind the phenomena for his bending of metal and telepathic powers. Controversy continues to rage as to how he does it, what trick he employs, and including downright condemnation that he is a fraud. No-one has been able to prove that his demonstrations are not the result of genuine psychic power. Until fraud is proved by responsible bodies such as scientists and researchers, the assumption must be that his powers are genuine.

Personally, I have no difficulty in accepting Uri Geller's abilities in this direction. He is simply demonstrating a force that is the same as that of any other physical mediumship which produces supernormal phenomena. The application of this force can be used in various ways for different purposes, as the examples cited in this book indicate. It may well be that the advent of Uri Geller will enable a breakthrough to be made where science accepts its responsibilities and ensures justice to those claiming to have supernormal powers.

However, the ability to bend knives and forks or influence any other objects by merely exercising mind power or psychic forces is not an end in itself. The true implications of these demonstrations will become more apparent with time, but at the moment they demonstrate that forces are active, governed by laws which we at present do not understand. The effect of these forces have been seen in one form or another for centuries, and history records the number of people who have been burned at the stake, murdered, hung, drawn and quartered, and even excommunicated from the Church because they possessed powers that were perfectly natural but were misunderstood and confused with superstition and sorcery.

The 'no-man's-land' between the conscious and unconscious mind is commanding more attention than ever before. Somewhere between these states lies the answer to many of the problems which psychic phenomena pose. The study of paranormal phenomena and investigations carried out by Professor Rhine of Duke University, North Carolina, USA, confirms the existence of extra-sensory perception, as do the experiments in Soviet Russia and other Communist countries in regard to psycho-kinesis (the movement of objects without human agency) plus the recent photographic evidence of the human aura.

Mediums have described the aura for years, using their clairvoyant faculties. Science rejected the idea until recently. Hypnotism encountered more opposition than anything else, but is now an accepted fact, the common property of psychology in the cure of nervous and stress diseases as well as an alternative to the use of anaesthetics in surgical operations.

The Scientific Approach to Investigation

All new discoveries have met with violent opposition and there is little reason to believe that psychic phenomena are an exception. However, it is my opinion that this new knowledge will find its place in the intellectual inheritance of mankind. The verdict as to the value of psychic phenomena in the advancement of knowledge, can be left to public opinion, as it, too, becomes enlightened.

Uri Geller presented an ideal opportunity for scientists, who have already indicated that they are prepared to investigate his powers, to make a serious study of the whole subject of supernormal activity. I should warn them, however, that their approach requires specific attention and it is vitally important that they consider the very special psychological conditions necessary to obtain the best results from those whom they are investigating. Mediums are extremely sensitive to the external attitudes of people towards them. A hostile and aggressive atmosphere is the quickest way to impede the psychic function of the medium's faculties and can easily lead to negative results.

Mediumship has its own essential conditions which must be respected and studied by the observer. Severe and excessive precautions to eliminate fraud can be carried to an extreme with a tendency to reduce phenomena. Therefore, a tolerant and humane method of investigation is required. So often in the past mediums have met with suspicion and ridicule that they have gone to ground rather than subject themselves to public scrutiny. The few that did so suffered untold humiliation and denigration.

Many Spiritualists, with their fanatical absence of criticism and incredulity, have hindered the education of mediums and their development because of their eagerness to witness phenomena at any price. This has served to render them quite blind to the distinction between facts explicable and those which are not. The methods of Spiritualists generally tend to encourage fraud because of their attitude in regarding mediums as saintly individuals venerated beyond all proportion. The fact that the best results have been obtained in the séance room, rather than in the laboratory, indicates that psychological conditions are of primary importance. Conjurors and magicians are not subject to rigorous investigation or search and permit no interference with the performance or experiments. In the case of the medium, all this is reversed. As soon as phenomena occur the medium is subject to the malicious, hostile or frivolous mentality of his audience, crying fraud and trickery to justify it.

A medium should never be regarded as fraudulent until the phenomena is proved to be so, just as in English law a person is innocent until proven guilty. The Spiritualist, in accordance with his religious habit of thought, retains only that which is essential to his belief. The sceptic will see fraud where none exists; the believer will see manifestations of spirits where conjuring tricks exist. Where people are committed to a decided point of view of the phenomena, favourable or unfavourable, it is difficult to obtain unprejudiced and objective determination. One thing is certain, a positive instance of genuine phenomena cannot be refuted by a thousand negative ones!

The main problem for the investigators is to devise a method for the examination of mediumistic processes that will provide free and uninhibited conditions, while at the same time ensuring that the test conditions are sufficient to establish the authenticity of the phenomena. It is important that benevolence is shown toward mediums so that they can attune their mentality to the special conditions of the experiments. The success of ESP tests is bound up with the mood, the confidence and undisturbed mentality of the medium. Suppressed suspicion or indifferent treatment can easily put the instrument out of tune. Fanaticism for exactitude can, in fact, lead to the drying up of the fountain altogether, so that the source for material and knowledge becomes non-existent.

As I see it, the fundamental rule should be that all conditions, controls, interference and experiment should, as far as possible, be arranged in such a way that the play of the medium's powers and the psychic performance as such are not hindered or interrupted in their development or mode of action, even at the risk of being accused of superficial and uncritical behaviour. Too rigid control of the conditions laid down can place the results in jeopardy. The wise investigator will secure the emotional state of the medium and avoid strain, as well as conserve nervous and psychic energy.

Mediumistic activity can be compared with the artistic capacity of creative power which is influenced by the surrounding physical conditions. Probably this is the reason why sittings in Spiritualist circles in which the medium is regarded with a measure of awe, are often more successful than so-called scientific sittings. It becomes obvious, therefore, to see that those who are engaged in the scientific investigation of mediumistic phenomena have an appreciation of the sensitive and abnormal nature of mediums.

The attitude directed toward the Uri Geller phenomena by various professional and rival groups such as magicians, conjurors and psychologists is nothing new and it would indeed be a mistake to allow them free licence to express opinions in the presence of the medium. A botanist does not presume to judge on astronomy! The main reason for the opposition from professional entertainers could be because they fear the possibility of the phenomena to be genuine and therefore a threat to their position. The fact their performance depends on skill and trickery would be regarded as subordinate or inferior to the performance of phenomena through a genuine medium. Jealousy, suspicion and ignorance all combine to adversely affect the results of a medium's performance.

All that is required for success is an open mind and a tolerant understanding, together with an honest determination to seek the truth. Everything should be done toward this end.

Investigations in the future will have to be conducted with a much greater respect for the medium than has been shown in the past, if positive results are to be obtained. Without the full co-operation of the medium, science cannot expect to gain any useful information, so it is essential for mutual respect to exist between the two. The opportunity is now open for full scale advancement toward learning more of this new science, with all its implications and possibilities. Science, too, appears to be better disposed today toward the reception and examination of new phenomena, however strange or absurd they may appear.

The purely materialistic conception of the Universe is slowly being abandoned as modern physics regards matter as a form of motion, dominated by the idea of energy. It will be interesting to see, under controlled conditions, the direct effect of psychic forces interacting between laws governing matter.

What I have witnessed in the séance room may be as nothing compared to what is possible under careful and wise scientific supervision and control, providing the scientists maintain a high standard, having regard to the points I have outlined with regard to the psyche of the human being. After all, man is the greatest computer so far devised, with unlimited potential.

Chapter 4

Spiritual Healing

Of all psychic phenomena, healing must surely rank amongst the most rewarding. Its purpose is clear and undeniable, providing irrefutable evidence of a superior intelligence at work. When treatment is effective as a result of psychic or spiritual healing, particularly in the case of a recognisable 'incurable' condition, one must accept that forces are operative outside and beyond our normal understanding. As with various other phenomena, the same challenge to science exists.

The extraordinary results being obtained by spiritual healers and psychic surgeons must inevitably raise many questions in the minds of people who encounter the subject, as to how and why spiritual healing works. Firstly, it is necessary to define the term spiritual healing and then attempt to remove some of the age-old misconceptions which surround its practice.

After many years' experience of this form of healing, as well as an intensive study of its practitioners, I would define it as the art of applying law-governed forces to bring about the reversal of an ill condition. These forces are as real and consistent as the law of gravity, but because physical properties of a chemical nature are required to assist the healing process, a human instrument is necessary in order for them to be intelligently transmitted from the healer to the patient. Everyone can benefit from the correct application of healing forces, regardless of sect, religion or ideology.

Spiritual healing does not require faith on the part of the patient – if faith was a requisite of healing, babies and animals would not respond as they do. Therefore, the commonly used term 'faith healing' is not only erroneous but irrelevant. A healer may or may not be a religious person since results indicate that it is not dependent upon a particular belief. Most of the healers I know are not religious in an orthodox sense. What they do have in common is a sincere desire to help sick people and a natural sympathy toward suffering. They also have the ability to avoid becoming emotionally involved with their patients so as to conserve nervous energy.

To be a healer, one does not need to wear a collar back to front, neither is it necessary to possess degrees, diplomas or certificates to qualify. The test of any 'healership' is in the results that are achieved, rather than how much one may talk about it!

Essentially, the healer must possess an abundance of psychic energy in addition to a particular chemistry that when combined with the patient's bodily healing mechanism triggers off and accelerates the patient's own healing processes. The patient is, in fact, on the receiving end of a power transmitted through the healer. Comparatively very few people have this 'gift' of transmission. Like great painters or musicians, it would appear that they are equally rare.

While it is not possible at the present time to know all the answers regarding the mystery behind the various phenomena of the psychic world, it is already becoming established scientifically that forces exist which man was completely unaware of only a few years ago. Research being carried out in the United States and the Soviet Union already indicates the reality of the human aura, a radiation which surrounds the body that for many years was only discernible by a clairvoyant. However, a series of colour photographs was recently produced under laboratory conditions using a special complex camera which records this radiation in various shades. It has been known for a long time by mediums who have been able to see the aura, that the colours indicate the physical and mental state of the person which it surrounds. Therefore, it is possible to diagnose a particular condition of health by 'reading' the aura. But a spiritual healer is not a doctor; he does not presume to diagnose, prescribe drugs or physics, neither would the Law allow it, since a healer is not usually medically qualified.

Most people seek the help of a healer only when the medical practitioner can do no more for them. Many patients are in a chronic state by the time the healer is asked to help. Yet so often when one of these cases is treated successfully, the medical comment is usually one of mistaken diagnosis or recession!

It would seem to be of little use that the medical profession continues to ignore the claims of healers simply because it cannot explain the results. What is even more important is the fact that spiritual healing does not oppose medical practice, it is complementary to it. If the skill of medical science was to combine with the forces of healing, I am firmly of the opinion that we should see less stress conditions, a reduction in psychosomatic illness and the end of many so-called incurable conditions and diseases.

It is an accepted fact that many drugs produce side effects often more distressing to the patient than the condition for which they are given. It would appear senseless to administer a drug in order to ease one condition only to bring about another! The dilemma of the medical profession is that it has concentrated on the physical aspect of the human body to the exclusion of the mental or spiritual. It has been a case of treating the symptoms rather than getting down to the cause, which is so often beyond the bounds of medical science.

A question frequently asked is, why do some people respond to spiritual healing better than others? It is not so much a matter of attitude on the part of the patient in so far as they may be sceptical or even ignorant of the subject. The measure of response is dependent upon various factors which govern the laws of healing. For instance, where surgery has been carried out and a vital nerve has been severed, it is most unlikely that spiritual healing can reconstruct what has in fact been destroyed; likewise the amputation of a limb.

There are no miracles in healing, all operates within the laws governing its practice and no matter how much we desire a cure for a particular condition, the laws cannot be reversed to suit our demands.

It is simply our lack of knowledge and understanding which causes us to look at the results of healing with awe and amazement.

In the past, much mumbo jumbo was associated with healing, either through evangelists or charlatans using methods and rituals which served only to bring the subject into disrepute. Many undesirable practices have proved to be entirely irrelevant and totally unnecessary. Simplicity is the keynote of healing. It requires only that the patient and healer combine in attunement. Whatever the factors which produce a small number of negative results, one is bound to weigh the greater number of successes against the failures. A figure of 80% is not unusual where a competent healer is able to induce a change for the better. No healer with a sense of modesty or humility would claim to be God! Some people respond quickly while others require successive treatments in order to progress.

It is important for the patient to realise their own contribution to the healing process and to avoid underestimating their capacity to share some of the credit for a successful healing. While the healer provides the opportunity for the necessary stimulus, chemistry and corrective energies, the patient should quietly accept this and register certain effects such as a warm, pleasant feeling or the desire to lapse into a drowsy half-sleep. Such effects indicate that the body is relaxed and receptive to the healing forces. It is at this point that certain chemical changes are induced to help to remove the offending condition.

A typical example of this can be seen in the case of arthritis where the joints are stiff as a result of salts and deposits collecting around them. In order for movement to be restored, it is necessary to disperse these deposits. Spiritual healing can achieve this quickly and painlessly within a very short time of the healer placing his hands upon the patient.

Sceptics often dismiss spiritual healing as mere suggestion, but if this were the case, then why is it not more widely used by the medical profession? If wishful thinking could remove a malignant growth, the problem of cancer would disappear overnight! The acceptance of the efficacy of spiritual healing will be fostered in the minds of those who have benefited from it. These are the people who, having been successfully treated, will testify to the truth in the final analysis. Once it has been accepted by the people, no force or body will be able to oppose it, for it will take its place among the other sciences which exist for the benefit of mankind.

Finally, it should be stressed that no healer can ever guarantee a cure – neither should a patient cease to receive medical treatment from their doctor while being treated by a healer.

There is much more to the subject of spiritual healing than we at present know and many of the questions it poses are still a matter of speculation. Yet the fact that extraordinary results continue to be evident is surely a sufficient reason to justify not only its wider acceptance, but its further development and ultimate recognition by all those concerned with the well being of people and who wish to see the end of so much needless suffering in the world.

At this point, it is pertinent to quote from a talk given by White Eagle, the spirit guide who manifested through me over a number of years. Dealing specifically with the subject of healing, he declared:

"The healing of the sick is the most important need in your world today. It is the noblest act of service you can give. To develop and practice the healing gift is the duty of all who dedicate their lives in service on behalf of human suffering.

"An instrument of healing must consider the needs of the patient above all else and refrain from anything that would impede the flow of healing power. Many of the failures and disappointments in healing arise through ignorance of the special requirements applying to its practice. Firstly, you must forget yourself, there is no room for self in service. Secondly, it is important to adopt a complete sense of humility – to proceed on assumptions or preconceived ideas is wrong. And thirdly, the qualities demanded are honesty, sincerity and complete confidence in the healing intelligence to transmit and direct healing forces to the patient.

"To be used as an instrument of healing is a privilege. It cannot be bought by the payment of a subscription or by resorting to any verbal formula or ritual. No one can pretend to understand the reality of the power that brings healing because none of us is sufficiently skilled in our knowledge to comprehend the source or intelligence behind the healing act. The ultimate test of healing is the result one obtains rather than how much one may talk about it!

"Your duty as an instrument of healing is to become a perfect channel, expressing love in your daily life and being the cause of unity among men. It must always be your aim to rise to the highest in your endeavours, be free from prejudice and keep an open mind. In pursuing your task, you must not allow your ego to supersede your common sense. The fact that healing forces manifest through many people, despite the varying conceptions they hold, shows that none must be so dogmatic as to believe they alone possess the truth.

"There will come a day when the work of healing will be concerned primarily with the prevention of disease rather than its treatment. Disease originates in the mind and if we can direct our attention to the cause, we shall avoid having to treat organic afflictions."

Whatever you may think about spirit guides or the source of the matter conveyed, if it enlightens us in our search for truth, then a purpose is served.

Harry Edwards – A Tribute

To anyone who has the desire to take up healing work, I can think of no better advice or guidance than that offered in the books by Harry Edwards, one of the greatest expounders and demonstrators of healing in this century. I have watched this man demonstrate to thousands of people in most of the largest halls in the country. I have seen him free locked joints in just a few moments. Patients suffering from slipped discs able to bend down and touch their toes without pain, cases of goitre smoothed away in seconds, poker back spines straightened and all manner of conditions responding to the healing forces transmitted through him to the patient.

In England and throughout the world there are numerous healing organisations, the largest being the National Federation of Spiritual Healers with a Registered membership of over 8,000 practicing healers. Harry Edwards, its Founder and President for many years, has done more for the cause of spiritual healing than any other man I know. Through his inspired efforts, he laid down a guideline for the future expansion and success of healing.

It is impossible to measure the unique contribution that Harry Edwards gave in the service of his fellow man. His invaluable knowledge and wisdom, both in his healing work and the advancement of psychic science, will come to be regarded with the same importance as those of other great pioneers in history. His dedication and love for humanity is expressed in the life-long service he has given, earning for himself a special place among the great men this world has produced through the centuries. To have met this wonderful man is to have met a giant! I doubt if the world will see the like of him again.

Harry Edwards, the internationally known healer,
pictured holding some of the six hundred letters from
doctors seeking help.

The Blacksmith who became a Healer

John Cain lived in the village of Eastham, south of the Wirral peninsula in Merseyside. John was a blacksmith by trade but gave up his business in order to devote his full time to healing the sick. During his service in H.M. Forces, John was a physical training instructor. Later, he obtained his Black Belt in Judo. He openly admitted that he was not a religious man in the orthodox sense, but he did recognise a Superior Intelligence. Most evenings he spent a quiet half hour with his wife in the local pub at about ten o'clock. He liked his pint!

His interest in healing was aroused as a result of an experience he had while sitting quietly in the pub. For about fifteen minutes he 'saw' a shimmering mass that he described as some kind of energy. We discussed this together and concluded that it was a sign that he had a gift involving a particular psychic faculty. As healing was his main concern, it was decided to put it to the test by treating his own daughter, Jeanette. Jeanette had about a hundred warts down the front of one of her legs. I saw these and could testify to their prominence. However, John simply placed his hand on the affected part of the leg. With each day, the warts diminished in size. Eight days later, they were completely gone.

Remarkable as this may seem, John reserved his judgment, even suggesting that it could be explained as a co-incidence. More patients were sought in order to confirm whether or not he did indeed have healing powers.

Patient number two was a gentleman suffering from multiple sclerosis, a progressive disease affecting the mobility of the spine, the limbs and adversely reducing vision in both eyes. It is a condition regarded as incurable by the medical profession. However, after only one visit by John, the sight of one eye was restored. Following four further visits to the patient, the strength and grip in the hands improved, movement in the legs was restored to the point where the patient was able to stand on his own feet!

The third case involved myself. For some years I had suffered from back trouble as a result of a prolapsed disc, and although I had hospital treatment, traction etc., hardly a day would pass without feeling a dull nagging ache. John came to see me and we discussed his potential healing powers. I told him about my back trouble and he responded by placing his hands on the affected spot. From that moment, I have not suffered any further trouble.

Probably the most challenging case was that of my wife, Irene. After having a stroke and being admitted to hospital, it was diagnosed that a severe cerebral haemorrhage had occurred. I was informed that no assurance could be given as to her recovery; if there was to be such, it might take a very long time. Complete loss of mobility and speech meant that there was no possible way of communicating with her.

I asked John if he would accompany me to the hospital each evening. This he did willingly and on each occasion, all he did was to hold my wife's hands. After three days, her speech returned and the use of her limbs was restored. Seven days later, she was discharged. No drugs or medical treatment had been given since the hospital staff were still undecided how to treat her. They were waiting for any change that might help them decide on the kind of treatment to give. As it was, the medical staff were amazed at her recovery.

There is case of the eighty-five-year-old lady who suffered with chronic arthritis (see picture on next page), who had been given up as incurable and told by her doctor that she must learn to live with it. This dramatic picture illustrates the result of a few moments of spiritual healing with John Cain after which she was able to raise her arms above her head for the first time in twenty five years. I saw so many others respond to the healing effort of John hat it was quite clear that he had a gift to heal. I saw a young man being treated for a stomach ulcer. That same patient returned to say that he was no longer in pain and was eating normally for the first time in two years.

An 85-year-old lady pictured with the late John Cain.
A sufferer from chronic arthritis after spiritual healing.
(Photograph by the Author)

Finally, there is Malcolm, another dystrophy patient. Since healing commenced, this boy put on weight and his muscles, instead of continuing to waste away, developed. His ambition was to be a footballer! That is positive thinking for you!

There are many more cases I could quote. The examples I have given illustrate the extraordinary power of spiritual healing. Unfortunately, healers are not as common as one would suppose. Relatively very few have the ability to heal. Perhaps it would not do for us all to be doctors, musicians, engineers or scientists.

As I have already explained, spiritual healing is complementary to medical practice just as all other activities are related in some way or other to combine in providing our society with its various needs.

Spiritual Hypnosis

A unique development to emerge as a result of John Cain's healership was the introduction of a new phenomenon described as Spiritual Hypnosis.

The effect of this new technique is to induce within the patient a trance-like state without any verbal suggestion on the part of the healer. With general hypnosis, the repetitive suggestion of the hypnotist is essential to put a subject to sleep prior to making the necessary verbal instructions required to bring about a specific result. In the case of a patient receiving spiritual healing where the new method is applied they are subject to a direct influence of the spirit guide or [spirit] doctor which serves to induce greater receptivity and consequently, allows the healing forces to be used with increasing effect.

I have watched several cases where people, quite independent of each other, succumb to this influence without a word passing from the healer. It is during the healing treatment that a phenomenon takes place which can only be described as a form of remote control where the patient's brain mechanism is manipulated in some way to produce involuntary movement of a limb or other part of the body. This movement is observable and appears to be outside the control of the patient and although conscious of it, they are unable to resist it.

In my opinion, after observing healing and other such varieties of psychic phenomena, we see here a direct control to influence the patient, independent of the healer. A typical example of the way this operates is given as follows. A patient having suffered a severe stroke was unable to move the right arm. During the healing process, this patient raised her right arm and from the wrist, began to rotate it at such speed that the hand was hardly visible. One has to see this vigorous reflex action to appreciate the spectacular nature of the phenomena.

There is little doubt that the therapeutic value of this effect serves a double purpose. First, it shows to the patient that a limb they believe to be immobile is not in fact so. Secondly, the patient is encouraged to look confidently toward progress and normality, through the healing process.

Psychic Surgery

While the mechanics behind the healing act remain very much a mystery, it is my belief that the forces are basically the same as for those governing all kinds of psychic phenomena.

In the case of psychic surgery, it would appear that there is a close connection with physical mediumship where dematerialisation of matter and vice versa, takes place. This principle applies where the dispersal of salts and deposits is necessary before a patient suffering from chronic arthritis is relieved of pain and mobility restored.

The dispersal of tissue or the displacement of the flesh by a psychic surgeon as he kneads his fingers to go inside the body is one of the most remarkable aspects of this form of healing. Without the use of knives or anaesthetic, the patient is opened up, the offending condition removed and as the 'surgeon' removes his hands from the patient's body at the end of the 'operation' the incision or wound closes up, leaving no mark or scar. Many of these operations would, if carried out in a hospital using orthodox surgery, take up to two or more hours with all the attendant paraphernalia, postoperative shock, possible complications, and invariably a long period of convalescence. In the case of psychic surgery, the patient is treated in usually about two or three minutes, getting up and walking away quite normally. They are usually fully conscious throughout the operation.

Several people, including doctors, have been to the Philippines and observed, filmed and recorded their observations. The reports are striking and a challenge to orthodox medicine.[1]

---

1. *See page 106 for more on this subject.*

Chapter 5

Psychic Development

Everyone is endowed with psychic faculties, whether they are aware of them or not. In most people they remain dormant simply because the mind is not directed toward their development. It is my belief that the true purpose of these faculties has not yet been fully realised and the exercise of them by mediums demonstrates only their limited use. So far, the development of the psychic faculties has been mainly confined to Spiritualists, whose chief purpose is to establish communication with the spirit world.

It may well be that a purpose other than this will emerge as man's intelligence increases. With a responsible and carefully controlled scientific approach to the whole question of psychic science, I believe we shall see much of the negative attitudes and ignorance surrounding the subject removed, giving way to a more enlightened view. The various superstitious practices of witchcraft, black magic and other occult lore will be seen for what they are: mere fringe rituals bound by irrelevant and trivial nonsense appealing to the ignorant and psychologically unstable.

The pursuit of matters relating to the occult is an ever increasing pastime as well as a lucrative occupation for charlatans and 'spivs', who conceive all manner of ways in which to foster on an ignorant section of society, 'readings', 'horoscopes', and what have you.

The practice of mediumship through which information pertaining to the future is obtained and the ability to produce phenomena beyond the normal range of human understanding is only now, after centuries, being seriously considered as worthy of attention by the scientific world. Medical science is becoming increasingly aware of the efficacy of psychic and spiritual healing, otherwise how is it that permission is now granted by no less than 1,500 hospitals in Britain for spiritual healers to treat patients, providing the doctor and nurse in charge of the ward are approached and the patient makes a request for spiritual healing?

One has only to examine the work of a man like Harry Edwards to realise the overwhelming evidence that spiritual healing provides. The testimony of countless numbers of people who have benefited from such treatment ensures a sound basis upon which future research can build. This will enable everyone to take advantage of psychic and spiritual forces which exist to eradicate sickness and disease.

If for no other reason, psychic development as a means of helping the sick must, of necessity, be of paramount importance in usefully directing the forces and energy previously used for trivial and less meaningful purposes.

In the past it has been left to the layman to propagate and encourage psychic development, but I feel the time has come for a complete reappraisal of the situation. The subject is too important to be left any longer in the doldrums, where trial-and-error alone has been the dominant factor. Instead, a carefully organised effort, backed by the resources of science, is vital.

Mediumship demonstrates something of the extraordinary powers man is capable of. That so little of the phenomena is understood is simply due to the fact that few people have been able to witness it. It is also understandable why scepticism persists towards mediums, since in the past, only the frauds received the publicity! The genuine phenomena of levitation, telekinesis, apports and other physical phenomena of the séance room have served to indicate that law governed forces operate beyond our present knowledge.

That these phenomena are means to an end rather than an end in themselves is obvious.

There must surely be a more purposeful use for such energies. If the collective effort of a few people in the presence of a physical medium can enable a piano to lift several feet from the floor, without any physical contact – and I have seen this happen – then it might explain the mystery of how the pyramids were built! It is a question of finding the best possible way of using these forces to benefit mankind rather than providing entertainment for a few sitting in a darkened room.

Again, my own experience of the methods employed by Spiritualists in the development of psychic faculties leaves a great deal to be desired. There is often a complete lack of discipline with the blind leading the blind. The whole thing is a hit or miss affair where many would-be mediums graduate to little more than mediocre speakers and demonstrators.

Others suffer from inflated egos once they have become 'recognised' as platform workers. The standard is poor and the audiences sparse but the situation continues to decline simply because of the lack of correct and competent guidance. The only reason for the dearth of physical mediumship is because it is no longer being developed. It is suggested that 'philosophy' is more important but I suspect that this is merely an excuse to cloud the issue and avoid facing up to the strict demands required for the development of physical mediumship.

The new custodians of psychic science will replace the amateurs and self-styled demagogues who have monopolised so much time in the pursuit of their own interests rather than in the search for truth. New methods based on sound lines, intelligently applied, may require revolutionary changes in the technique regarding the development of the psychic faculties. In view of the fact that science has little scope as yet for measuring psychic forces, it will be a case of having to begin its research by using methods totally different from those applying to normal physical science.

Experiment and research must be conducted with discipline, patience and understanding if science is to cut through the morass of irrelevance at present associated with the subject. Mediums of high repute should be encouraged to co-operate in detailed experiment with scientists, providing, of course, that mutual respect exists and honesty and sincerity are the criteria. In this way, the road is open to progress and fulfilment, to meet the need of mankind materially, psychically and spiritually.

Mediumship can be divided into two separate categories, physical and mental, the former being used primarily to effect physical changes such as is required in the case of organic disease. Psychic operations would replace surgery. The implication behind this is obvious, since there would be enormous financial savings as well as the complete absence of post-operative shock and the long period of convalescence required after major surgery.

Psychic or spiritual healing is clean, safe, quick and painless. The surgeon's knife will be regarded by future generations as both clumsy and primitive as a more sophisticated method of healing is applied, without the disadvantages or risks at present involved. The psychic operations at present carried out are themselves open to question and doubt, but as the early Marconi wireless set is a far cry from the modern hi-fi stereo, so will psychic surgery develop until it becomes acceptable to modern requirements.

The healing potential of certain human beings is already an established fact, when this is harnessed and put to use in a positive way, then I believe we shall see a revolution in medicine as we know it today. In the Philippines, there are one or two mediums carrying out psychic operations for the removal of tumours and cancerous growths, as well as other conditions where normal surgery would be required. The techniques adopted come within the category of physical mediumship. Although a great deal of controversy surrounds this kind of phenomenon, it is quite evident the same challenge presents itself to both the medical and scientific world.

A typical example of the way one of these operations is performed has already been given in the previous chapter.

A friend of mine has recently returned from the Philippines where both he and his wife underwent operations with one of these mediums. He was fortunate in being able to film several operations in colour. Whether or not this kind of surgery will ever be accepted in the West is dependent on the ability of psychics to develop it. As I have already stated, there is a great deal of scepticism as well as horror with regard to the methods and techniques practised by some Brazilian and Filipino psychic surgeons.

The whole process, while extraordinary, is still primitive and it is my belief that it could be developed to a finer degree. For instance, I saw an operation in Cardiff, South Wales, several years ago where a Welsh medium removed an appendix from a patient without even touching the body. Being a physical medium, such things are possible, providing the medium's development is sufficiently strong enough to allow for supernormal dispersal of diseased tissue from the body.

I have indicated a primary use for psychic energy as it applies to physical mediumship for the purpose of treating the sick. What useful purpose mental mediumship can offer is an open question. Generally, Spiritualists put the emphasis on the practice of clairvoyance, attributing most, if not all, the information gained to the intervention of discarnate agencies. In its widest sense, clairvoyance is the ability to 'see' people, places and events relating to the past and the future. Precognition, psychometry, crystal gazing, etc., all come under the category of mental phenomena. Telepathy, in my opinion, plays a greater part in mental mediumship than many people would admit. The fact that so much of the information given by mediums is already contained within the memory of the recipient, leads me to suspect that this information is readily available to any medium who is sensitive.

That is not to suggest fraud, but an unconscious element by which insufficient attention is directed in determining whether the information comes from the subconscious mind of the recipient, or emanates from a discarnate source. Whatever the truth, it is quite obvious that a faculty exists where mind can commune with mind. As to being able to 'see' future events, good or bad, it is in this direction that I believe the human race could benefit from such a faculty. Again, it is wholly dependent on a highly developed medium.

In the past, countless examples of precognition have gone unheeded, the result being that many lives have been lost that could have been saved had the warnings been recognised and certain precautions taken. The evidence of a foolproof method of foretelling future events is fragmentary but sufficiently strong to indicate that there is room for improved methods of research. World events such as the weather, hurricanes, earthquakes, droughts, etc., have all at some time or other been pre-cognised by people. If such people were trained and developed to a high degree, they would be an invaluable asset to the community.

Disasters arising from human error such as plane crashes, rail disasters, deliberate acts of sabotage, murder and assassination are all events that are capable of being pre-cognised. The old saying, 'to be forewarned is to be forearmed', is more than applicable in many of these cases. Recognition of the value of information acquired through the psychic senses in order to meet contingencies of this nature would serve in future to avoid many tragedies of the past.

Returning to the situation within the Spiritualist movement, I have seen many changes in the character of the phenomena demonstrated, particularly in healing methods where many practices are now discounted as being irrelevant. The fact that in the past certain results were obtained, was not because of these practices, but in spite of them. Again, in the case of physical mediumship, many aspects, such as lighting in the séance room, prove that it is no longer essential to conduct the proceedings in total darkness. I have witnessed excellent physical phenomena in good red light as well as diffused white light. I believe in the past, that many of the conditions demanded by mediums depended to a large extent upon the way they developed in the beginning.

The strong belief that white light was an impediment to the production of physical phenomena, was more a matter of education than anything else. The medium's apprehensions toward light were, in my opinion, based on ignorance or fear. Recent demonstrations of physical phenomena in white light indicate that such fears or apprehensions on the part of the medium arose from a mental condition, probably more psychological than based on reason and fact. The physical phenomena demonstrated by Uri Geller on television demand the use of brilliant lighting in the studio. Never once was it suggested that such conditions were unsuitable for the phenomena to occur. Transfiguration of a medium's features where red light is used has also been proved to be unnecessary. I have seen transfiguration in good white light. Again it is a matter where the education of the medium plays a part during the early developing period.

With regard to the development of the psychic faculties, it is important to decide and ascertain the purpose which motivates the desire for such development. If the intention is a good one, it is essential that the individual acquires as much knowledge of the powers and forces involved as possible.

To commence psychic development ignorant of the pitfalls can result in frustration and disappointment. So many of the failures in Spiritualist 'circles' are due to the lack of competent leadership, patience and a constructive approach. Discipline, too, is an important factor, the lack of which encourages sitters to resort to all manner of trivial exhibitions, resulting in a pantomime atmosphere serving no useful purpose whatsoever. If the subject is to be regarded with any respect at all and the interest of scientific bodies encouraged, then it is vital that the standard of mediumship is improved.

The need to prop up religious belief is not a justification for psychic development. One does not need to be a religious person to become an accomplished musician or a doctor. The sooner psychic science is regarded in the same way, where a clairvoyant is recognised not as the property of the Spiritualist movement but as an asset to the community in general, then it is most likely such gifted people will gain wider recognition than they have in the past.

Chapter 6

Some Personal Views and Observations

Having regard to the phenomena I have been fortunate to observe over many years, I am bound to admit their reality. As I have said, it is one thing to describe something but another to explain it. Unless one has had first-hand experience of a particular subject, it is impossible to appreciate the truth concerning it. This is, of course, understandable, especially where such a highly complex and controversial subject as psychic phenomena is concerned. On the other hand, there are some people so totally ignorant of these things, and in spite of their lack of knowledge continue to pontificate and express opinions, proving nothing but their own inferiority.

It always amazes me how far intellectuals will go to denounce or explain away that which they cannot understand. I suspect that their pride prevents them from admitting they simply do not know. Criticism is better coming from those who have seen and examined the evidence and obtained some knowledge of the mechanics of mediumship, its psychology and purpose.

The suspicions directed toward mediumship and attempts at negative explanations by 'experts' will continue as long as ignorance of the subject exists. Spiritualists should aim at a higher standard and show a little more discrimination between the performances of mediums in general. Far too much irrelevant material is accepted as 'evidence' when it is merely the result of guesswork, fishing, padding and downright fabrication. If more people were to demand a better standard, many practising mediums doing platform work would be driven back to the developing circle from which, unfortunately, they made a premature exit.

I recently witnessed a public 'transfiguration' session where the audience comprised a majority of elderly ladies who were obviously sincere, but frankly, it was pathetic to see these people being exploited by a 'medium' who gave nothing whatsoever in the way of 'evidence'. To rely on the dramatic setting of a red light shining on one's face in a sea of surrounding darkness is not enough. No doubt the few pounds obtained by the 'medium' for his performance would give him some satisfaction but it would do little for the prestige or reputation of the church in which the meeting was held.

Another example of deception involved a friend of mine. He came to see me one day, accompanied by his wife, to ask me if I would psychometrise an 'apport' which they had received at a séance. He told me nothing about the reason for his visit except to place in my hand a small stone. "Tell me what you get with that," he said. After a few moments I began to relay my impressions. "The stone has no significance whatsoever, it is one that might have been picked up on the shore," I said. Suddenly, I saw (clairvoyantly) a hand throw or toss the stone into a small area where three people were present, and stated so. Then I saw the person who threw the stone! "My God!" I remarked to my friend, "I know who it was," and turning to my friend's wife, who had a half smile on her face, I said "You know who I mean, it was so-and-so. "Yes," she replied almost reluctantly. For a moment there was a silence.

What was extraordinary about this is that the 'medium' through whom the alleged 'apport' appeared during a sitting in darkness was regarded very highly as a trance medium. Such attempts to 'produce' phenomena, even by genuine mediums, is a sign of their failing powers. In this particular instance, the medium in question had to my knowledge never developed the ability to produce physical phenomena and I could only feel very sad that he should try to 'pull a fast one' on a friend who sincerely regarded him with respect as a brilliant trance medium.

So far as mediums are concerned, a tremendous responsibility rests upon them to avoid the traps and pitfalls so often placed before them. Honesty and integrity is of primary importance where mediumship is concerned. I believe that one of the greatest dangers to mediums is when they become socially involved with some of their clients. The clients, on the one hand, can exploit a medium for their own ends, making severe demands on his 'gifts', so much so that the medium is stretched beyond his capacity. If this happens, then it is likely that the medium will resort to fraud in order to maintain his reputation.

As the old saying goes, 'Truth will out', and when it does, the confidence enjoyed between medium and client becomes tenuous as suspicion grows, until the friendship which started so promisingly descends to one of tolerant association, until final disillusionment.

One earlier experience when I visited a circle where physical phenomena purported to take place proved to be so blatantly fraudulent that the proceedings were, in fact, exposed by supernormal means! During the séance, which took place in complete darkness, a bright flash burst from the floor, illuminating the whole room. Standing as large as life in the centre of the floor was the 'medium' waving a trumpet! Pandemonium broke out. The séance ended abruptly. In his panic, the 'medium' dropped the celluloid trumpet which mysteriously caught fire and was destroyed. One of the sitters frenziedly stamped out the fire. Although the lino surface covering the floor had been subjected to a great heat, not a mark was visible when the surface was cleaned free of the charred remains of the trumpet! What had been clearly evident to all present was that the 'medium's' exposure appeared to result from the very forces he was attempting to imitate!

Fortunately, frauds are comparatively rare since they are unable to produce phenomena that would stand up to investigation. Only the incredulity of a minority enables such 'mediums' to function for a limited period before they are finally exposed one way or another. However, the scales tilt very much in favour of the genuine medium, whose reputation grows with the years.

Conclusion

Throughout this book, I have attempted to put forward a variety of aspects I believe to be relevant concerning the nature and underlying causes of psychic phenomena. While many of the views expressed may arouse controversy among Spiritualists, they are, nevertheless, sincerely held.

The claim that discarnate entities are responsible for the phenomena may be a true and valid one and the question is no longer whether these phenomena occur, because I believe it is a fairly well established fact. The question now remains: do they result from discarnate influences in a world outside that of the physical world, e.g., a spirit world, or is it possible that man himself in some mysterious way is responsible for producing the phenomena without realising it?

In the absence of exact proof, one is bound to accept the Spiritualist hypothesis, if only because any alternative theory in the light of our present knowledge maybe even more inexplicable! Where I tend toward deviation from the Spiritualist view is in the fact that I believe, from instinct rather than exact knowledge, that communication with the spirit world is not only extremely difficult but of rare occurrence.

For Spiritualists to attribute the phenomena of mediumship entirely to discarnate sources is to over simplify the problem. Just as science will have to change its view of the universe in view of their discoveries in psychic science, so do I believe that Spiritualists will have to modify many of their preconceived ideas about spirit communion and the after-life.

Things are not always what they seem to be, as time often proves. I am convinced that much of the phenomena of the séance room will be explained in a perfectly rational way as more becomes known with regard to man's innate potential.

Man has always looked to an abstract source to justify mysteries he is unable to understand. Even today, certain disasters are attributed to 'act of God'. Because our knowledge is so limited in these matters, the tendency has been to ignore them or to evolve explanations which fit in with our mode of belief. Orthodox religion, for instance, has survived for centuries based solely on faith, superstition, tradition and the fear of the devil. It is not surprising that as ignorance gives way to knowledge, the inevitable decline of the church continues.

Many may disagree with this view but what is the sense in bolstering an institution that has been so discredited with its history of murder, persecution and conflict? The fact which must be faced is that the church is nothing more than a financial and political organisation. The work of healing the sick is left to ordinary men and women – printers, blacksmiths and bus drivers, to name but a few. A remark by a Bishop in response to one of his clergy who requested that he have permission to hold healing services inside his church was as follows: "It may sound very well, but supposing I told you to try it and nothing happened?" – so much for practising what they have been preaching about for so long.

With a new approach to the investigation of the psyche, I believe that much will be uncovered concerning mediumship, leading to a better understanding of religion and the question of survival. With new conceptions, realised by scientific advances in the field of psychical research, the opportunity will be open for a man to take a further leap forward toward a better understanding of the universe of which he is an integral part.

What then is the future of psychic science? I believe that the supernormal faculties which man has demonstrated throughout history will find their true place. The study and development of these faculties will increase and form part of the curriculum in schools, colleges and universities in the same way as other subjects such as art, music, science and medicine. As the surgeon's knife becomes obsolete, so will drugs be a product of the past. Man will in fact begin to learn and understand the true nature of his being, the purpose for living and the meaning of death – not as an end, but a continuing cycle of activity. The challenge this presents to man will occupy his attention for many years to come.

The current obsession with materialism will give way to a more spiritual way of life, while the development of the psychic faculties will enable man to transcend the limitations of the physical body.

With the aid of the microscope, science has shown to us a world beyond our normal vision. Could it be that the psychic dimension is but an extension of the physical world, simply waiting to be discovered, providing a new energy and force to meet the need of a man as he progresses toward a new age?

There is little doubt that we are on the fringe of great new discoveries. Up till now, we have only been scratching the surface. This book has aimed at providing something of the evidence of that fringe, to suggest a better scientific approach to the investigation of psychic phenomena and point the way to a serious consideration about one of the most important subjects of modern times.

The great mistake now would be to ignore the matter, however complex it may be. Though man will ultimately unfold the secret and mystery of his psychic nature, this may well open the door to yet a further enigma concerning his true reality.

Chapter 7

The Last Twenty Years

This book so far relates to the years from 1943-1973 but the following twenty years were no less momentous.

Most of the time has been spent in promoting mediumship and healing. My home for instance has been used on a regular weekly basis for contact and absent healing – an important part of my life since 1958 when I first joined the National Federation of Spiritual Healers.

In 1983, I was invited to the home of Rita Lorraine Goold and her husband who then lived in the suburbs of Leicester. Rita was a physical medium. My week-long stay proved to be one of the most rewarding experiences during which my dear wife Renie who passed in 1979, materialised on five occasions, one of which was witnessed by a good friend of mine who knew my wife and often gave her healing.

One of the leading communicators at Rita's sittings was my old friend Helen Duncan, whom I knew on earth. I attended many of her materialisation séances prior to her passing in 1956, following a police raid from which she never recovered. To meet Helen again was indeed quite something. This twenty-two stone [308lbs/137.5kilos] woman sat next to me and gave me a bear hug I shall never forget. I remember thinking to myself: this was no spook or ghost; this was the solid form of the woman I knew.

She talked and reminisced about matters that took place in Liverpool thirty-five years previously, the same Perthshire dialect was sustained for about three quarters of an hour and I was left in no doubt it was my old friend, Helen. I wrote her biography *The Story of Helen Duncan* in

1975. The book has never gone out of print and continues to be in demand to this day as I write these words – August 20th 1993. What follows can only be described as one of the most traumatic events of my life. The promise of fulfilment, ending in disaster – or so I was to believe at the time.

As a result of a BBC Radio broadcast covering an hour-long programme, titled *The Last Witchcraft Trial* based on my book about Helen Duncan, I came to know 'Stewart'[1]. He had been touring Wales with his family and had heard the broadcast on his car radio. Stewart decided there and then to make contact with me. For several months we corresponded and then, in what appeared to be a coincidence, we met up at Leicester. Unknown to me, he had booked a sitting with Rita Lorraine Goold and I was to meet him on the day of my arrival when I spent the week at Rita's home.

Our meeting was the beginning of a friendship which lasted several years. Stewart had a circle near his home on Humberside and invited me there on a couple of occasions. Clearly, Stewart was a physical medium and was pursuing his development with promise. It was later that he travelled across the Pennines to my home near Chester and after some discussion, it was agreed that he come to my home each month and set up a circle where his development would continue.

For nearly six years I watched Stewart's mediumship develop. We had what I can only describe as the best bunch of sitters it was possible to assemble. Without doubt the sitters had been carefully chosen, blended well and proved that, with the right ingredients, we were to witness a variety of physical phenomena on a par with that of any of the pioneers of the past.

It had always been my aim to capture physical phenomena on film. In the past, so much had been lost by mediums being reluctant to allow a camera to record something of the phenomena that took place.

---

1. *Known to us now as Stewart Alexander, physical medium.*

The advent of the video camera brought what I believed to be the ideal means of capturing physical phenomena in all its stages, showing the process as it actually happens. It was an exciting prospect. Having regard to past efforts to persuade mediums to allow photography and the problems I encountered, I felt instinctively that Stewart may be the means for the great breakthrough.

We discussed it. It was put to 'White Feather', the medium's guide. To my surprise, the response was favourable. The idea of capturing phenomena on film via the video camera was to say the least an exciting one. This idea came to be known as 'The Project'.

The question of obtaining the video equipment plus the enormous cost occupied my mind; the prize of filming the phenomena for the very first time was an objective not to be missed. I wrote a letter to *Psychic News* calling for anyone interested in filming the phenomena of the séance room to make contact with me. Enter a young man named Simon Forsyth from Manchester. Simon wrote to me expressing his interest and informing me that he was hoping to obtain the equipment at any time.

I invited him to my home and we discussed matters. It soon became clear to me that this was no coincidence and was part of a 'plan'. Simon and I got on quite well. He was a member of the Society for Psychical Research and appeared to have a sound grasp of the subject. I discussed Simon with the sitters of the circle and suggested he joined the circle. Everyone agreed after meeting him and like a well-fitting glove he blended perfectly with the group. With the acquisition of the video equipment, Simon set up the camera at each subsequent sitting. Stewart's guide made references to the procedure to adopt and only when they were ready would instructions be given to switch on the camera.

In the meantime, progress was maintained and the phenomena – direct voice, levitation of the trumpet and other items, together with apports continued. Finally, materialisation was about to manifest. The mediumship had reached a peak of development. All was in place for The Project to proceed. Great patience had been exercised on the part of the sitters as the months passed with no positive progress so far as the filming was concerned.

Then came the assurance we had all waited for – White Feather expressed the wish that Spirit wanted to push ahead with the project, whilst at the same time stressing caution as regards the effect upon the medium's health and the pressures that may ensue from producing filmed evidence so far as the circle members were concerned. This was duly accepted and appreciated. It was however, encouraging to note that the spirit friends were anxious to co-operate – that being so, we settled back and left matters in their hands.

Increasing support for the filming of physical phenomena using the video camera was coming from within the various sections of the Spiritualist movement. The Spiritualist National Union was embarking upon providing a special room at Stansted Hall, the Arthur Findlay College in Essex, to promote physical mediumship. Suitable lighting and various other requirements were being installed as well as the eventual filming of physical phenomena. The Society for Psychical Research in London was also calling for progress in the field.

The Noah's Ark Society (NAS) for the promotion and safe practice of physical mediumship was formed in 1990 and its Chairman Robin Foy was an avid supporter in obtaining filmed evidence of psychic phenomena. It really did look as though things were moving in the right direction, with the Elton Circle in the forefront.

Our circle was host to many visitors who were able to witness phenomena for the first time in their lives. The news spread of what they had seen and heard in direct voice communications, the video project added spice as the Elton Circle was dubbed 'The Jewel in the Crown'.

All was in place. The years of patience and effort on both sides seemed about to be rewarded. However, I began to feel a distinct sense of unease. Several references to the project by Stewart's guides, White Feather and Old Jack (as he referred to himself) caused great concern.

The fears I and other members had for the circle began to increase. Eventually, it was my duty as Leader of the circle to express my own fears for the future of the project and indeed the very survival of the circle itself.

After much soul-searching and discussion, there was parting of the ways. The 'Jewel in the Crown' was plucked from us.

The disappointment remains but I have no doubt that materialisation in the séance room will be filmed, and in the not too distant future. I hope that at the very least, the Elton Circle, by its own development work, will be regarded as having contributed to its achievement.

Some time after the Noah's Ark Society for Physical Mediumship was formed, I was elected its President for two years but had to relinquish the position due to ill health. I have since resigned my membership of that organisation.

The loss of my circle and my total withdrawal from the NAS left a vacuum. However, this was filled immediately by a flood of activity beyond my wildest dreams. The final prophesy told me by Mrs Gunning back in 1946 was after all about to be realised concerning the propaganda work I would do – that was to give out the Truth as I understood it, based on the experience accumulated over the years.

Simon Forsyth was a valued member of the ill-fated Elton circle. I had told Simon about eighteen months previously that he had a role in psychic work. Despite his request to know what it was, I simply could not tell him, but that it would become clear to him in the not too distant future. I did get the month of May for him to watch for.

Then one day, Simon told me he was going to launch a new psychic newspaper and invited me to be its Features

Editor. Clearly, here was yet another outlet for the propaganda work Mrs Gunning had spoken of so many years before. In May 1993, Simon came to my home and deposited the first issue of *Psychic World* on my table. "Look at the publication date," he urged. It was May!

Simon is the founding editor of *Psychic World*. Its rapid success is due to sheer initiative and enthusiasm – with not a little help from Spirit...

The original editor and founder of *Psychic News*, Maurice Barbanell, made his influence felt and I told Simon I was convinced 'Barbie', as he was called, was behind the launch of the paper. In a strange kind of way, this was confirmed when Simon and myself went to London to see Tim Haigh, the then Editor of *Psychic News*. He said: "Where did you get the title for your newspaper?" "It came to me in a flash," I replied. "Well I must tell you that the first journal that Maurice Barbanell produced before *Psychic News* was called *PSYCHIC WORLD*!" Now that was over sixty years before and I knew nothing of the sort until I heard it from Tim.

As for my part, I am entering the twilight years and with failing health and strength; I have slowed up a lot. It has been a long journey and I have done my best. The worth of my life lies in the hope that it has helped somebody along the way.

My sincere gratitude to all my friends for their kindness to me.

Also to my dear wife Renie who has remained by my side since she passed and has looked after me. Finally, to the Shining Ones in Spirit whom I have endeavoured to serve during the last fifty years – thank you.

Post Script

The Author would like to say a word about Hems de Winter without whose help, advice and generosity this book may never have been published.

Hems knocked on my door a few months ago – "Alan Crossley?" he asked. "Yes," I replied. This very tall man then said: "I'm sorry to bother you: my name's de Winter." I didn't recognise him. For a moment, I was puzzled.

"Are you Hems?" I enquired and then all was clear. I remembered Hems when he was about thirteen years-of-age, and he was tall then. "Come in," I said, and then began a long discussion, including reminiscences of his mother Helen whom I knew quite well about twenty-five years ago.

I live in a mobile home with low ceilings. The fan was operating and when Hems' 6' 4" frame rose from his seat his head struck the blades and nearly decapitated him! Ever since, and to our mutual amusement, he moves about my home like the 'Hunchback of Notre Dame'!

Following a severe Angina attack, I had to ring Hems to cancel a meeting he had arranged, and told him of the attack. That morning my home seemed to fill with friends – amongst them was Hems, he brought several bags of fruit, tinned cream and fresh strawberries, tomato soups, cakes, cheese and so many other items I thought it was Christmas! Then together with a lady from Wales, he gave me some healing. I have to admit to feeling so well since then! How wonderful it is, to have such friends and for them to be there when needed.

Twenty-five years ago, Hems' mother invited my wife, Irene, and myself to visit her cottage in a remote spot in Wales. I remember it as one of the most idyllic settings I have ever been to. All those years later, Hems said to me, "Would you like to go to the cottage?" We went and spent a most enjoyable day there. The sound of the running stream by the side of the cottage was exactly as it was all those years before.

Again, with his newspaper experience, Hems has been of great assistance to Simon Forsyth, the Editor of *Psychic World*. His association with *Psychic World* will provide a useful contribution that will be very much appreciated.

Like a bolt out of the blue, Hems has transformed my life from the vacuum left following the collapse of the circle and having to resign my Presidency and membership of the Noah's Ark Society.

But for his kindness, *A Journey of Psychic Discovery* may never have been published. Words cannot express my sincere thanks and appreciation to him. But I know he is aware how grateful I am and pleased he thought my work worthy enough to go to such lengths, to get it published. Wonders never cease! Thank you, my dear friend.

> Alan Crossley took leave of his earthly life on 26th February 2001.

Hems de Winter
(publisher of the first edition)

It was at the age of about twelve that I first became aware of a publication called *Psychic News*. I used to find copies at our Wirral home and read them with avid interest. For a young man, they made fascinating reading! I became aware too that my mother had found a new interest.

Mum was involved in what I later understood to be a 'circle'. Occasionally, friends would come to the house on set evenings. More often than not, Mum simply 'went out'. It was not until many years later that I discovered she was developing as a healer and pursuing an interest in other psychic phenomena.

I do recall on one occasion making up the numbers at a 'table', a responsibly conducted ouija sitting. Instead of employing a glass, the sitters used a wooden cross with a point protruding from the centre. A sitter's index finger would rest on each arm of the cross. I well remember the impact on me of the energies which were manifest in moving the cross and its point around the board.

I received a number of messages. Even at such a young age, I remember feeling deeply impressed but strangely undaunted by what seemed to me to be perfectly natural experiences!

It was at this time I met healer, clairvoyant and public demonstrator Alan Crossley with his wife Irene. My earliest recollections of him were during their visit to our holiday cottage in North Wales. I met him on no more than two occasions before, temporarily as it turned out, he disappeared from my life.

'Uncle' Wout Kalis, a relative of my mother's, was another individual who played a role in my early life. I became close friends with his two sons and often stayed over at the family home in Wirral. I well remember our family's concern and support when Wout was involved in a terrible car accident which nearly cost him his life.

I knew little in those days but became aware that Uncle had withdrawn from his business life and, continuing to recover from his terrible injuries, moved to Belgium to become a healer on a full time basis.

A friend and I used to call in to see him *en route* to see my grandmother in Holland. On one of these visits, in 1983, Uncle Wout suggested during conversation that I should contact Alan Crossley at some time. He himself wrote Alan's address in my diary. I couldn't understand at that time why he made that suggestion, nor did I question it.

Not being a keeper of diaries, I used to throw each year's diary away. For some reason, I still have the 1982 diary. It seemed to surface on a regular basis and I remember on a number of occasions wondering why that name and address were even there! Perhaps Uncle Wout could see something even then?

Since those early years, my only 'contact' with Spiritualism has been one or two readings with clairvoyants and an occasional visit to a Spiritualist Church. Looking back, I can recall occasions when I have been aware of supernormal help and support. I simply took these for granted, overlooking their reality. I believed in a spirit dimension and was developing my own youthful ideas on the purpose of life. I didn't feel I needed to know more than that.

It wasn't until the beginning of 1993 that events took a course. There was something about an advert in the Chester Chronicle that inspired me. It advertised 'an evening of psychic discovery' at a hotel near my home.

I found myself desperately wanting to attend. However, personal commitments made this impossible. I was very disappointed. Later that week, in the subsequent edition of the *Chester Chronicle*, I happened to notice an entry in the Personal column. The clairvoyant from that event was advertising personal readings. I felt strongly motivated to book a reading and did so immediately.

A number of clairvoyant /mediums have told me over the years that I was psychic. The opening words of the reading were, "You could be doing what I'm doing." The reading was quite astonishing in its accuracy.

Comments about my future work with Spirit inspired me. Things began to fall into place. I felt elated at the prospect. Alan Crossley's name immediately sprang to mind. Was he still alive? Would he still be at the address I had? I felt a strong urged to contact Alan and seek his advice. As ever, the diary was nearby.

I decided to go and see him. Never before had I felt so strongly motivated to do something. I found his home with remarkable ease. There I was, standing on the doorstep of a man whom I had not seen for at least twenty-five years and who was unlikely even to remember me.

The warmth of welcome I received then has never faltered. Like many before me who have trod the path to Alan Crossley's door, I explained that I didn't really know why I was there but that I had been told on several occasions that I had some psychic ability. I wanted to be sure of this and, if it was the case, I needed guidance as to what to do about it. Could he perhaps help me? Deep down, I knew I was there for a reason. So did Alan.

Alan, who was still practicing as a healer, gave me the answers. Instead of making me feel as if I had disturbed his peace, he made me feel like a long lost friend.

Alan has guided me towards the greatest of all spiritual gifts, that of attunement. He has also taught me how to listen and how to 'wait on Spirit'.

With the help of those he has served so well in Spirit, he has helped me develop a gift of healing. He has taken pleasure in 'my' successes and encouraged me in my 'failures'. I am just one of many to whom Alan has given so freely and willingly of his time, providing advice, encouragement and the many benefits of his vast knowledge and experience.

Alan's influence on my development remains indispensable, as does the support and guidance I receive from John and Tracy Parkes, healer and medium respectively, to whom I was originally guided.

The purpose of recording these few personal comments is to illustrate how our spirit friends have so effectively planned and developed my role, as they have done and continue to do for so many others.

Alan Crossley continues to be a major influence in my development. It is in gratitude to him and the Spirit friends who have reacquainted us to further their purpose, that this book has been published.

I hope it may inspire others to 'listen' and seek their own truth.

H.W. de Winter.

Addendum

Foreword to
The Enigma of Psychic Phenomena

I am pleased to be associated with the dedication of this book *The Enigma of Psychic Phenomena* by my friend Alan Crossley to our mutual friend, John Kinsella, and so to more permanently testify to his life of devotion to spiritual healing through this book.

There is little doubt that today's generation are spiritually hungry, for there is little evidence to demonstrate the claims of Church theologies, of all kinds, that man is a spiritual being having a heritage of eternal life.

This book is a worthy contribution, especially to those who have no knowledge or experience of the psychic potential, to inform them of some of the ways psychic science proves beyond all reasonable doubt the truth that the members of the human family are akin to spirit in this life now.

Every case of spiritual healing and psychic phenomena is a planned act. To carry out a plan, an intelligence is needed, possessing the wisdom of knowing how to carry out the healing or the act.

As the healing of the so-called 'medically incurable' and the operation of other psychic gifts, are beyond the knowledge of doctors and scientists to perform, it proves the operating intelligences are not human and therefore are of Spirit.

Every act of change in our universe, results from the application of law-governed forces to the subject. There is no exception. So when the act of healing or manifestation of a psychic act, is purposely sought for, then it proves in our matter of fact age, that there is intelligent communication between intelligences from the spirit dimensions. Thus, spirit phenomena expressed through mediums and healers bring the two dimensions, spirit and physical, together in co-operative harmony.

As this book plays its part in making these truths more widely known, so it brings nearer the time when mankind will out-law the material, vicious, and ignoble codes of life, by which mankind struggles to live within unrest, poverty, hunger, wars and man striving against his fellows, and thereby himself.

No truth can be submerged forever, whether it be by the Church or medicine, the time has come when 'truth will out'.

Man is a spiritual being in this life now. Every act of spirit healing proves this, and his spiritualisation can only come from the amassing evidence that this life is but an apprenticeship for the greater life, which lies ahead of all of us. As this book fulfils its purpose in this effort so it will help the human family to secure for the children of tomorrow a happier heritage than that which we have known.

Harry Edwards

(1974)

Printed in April 2024
by Rotomail Italia S.p.A., Vignate (MI) - Italy